PENG

STRATEGY HUDDLE

Deepak Dhayanithy is associate professor of strategic management at IIM Kozhikode. He has been at IIM Kozhikode since 2011, offering and teaching elective courses to MBA and PhD students on sports, analytics, decision-making, poker and strategy. His research includes sports phenomena and the natural environment. During the first decade of this century, he completed his PhD (fellow, IIM Lucknow) and witnessed the unfolding of the subprime crisis from his perch in the subprime mortgages industry. In the 1990s he studied architecture and worked as an architect before turning to management studies. Born and raised near Elliot's Beach in Chennai, he spent an inordinate amount of time playing and following a range of sports and games. His academic writing includes research papers in sports contexts, book reviews for sports management journals and articles in news outlets. It is his understanding that there is more to sports than fun and games, and that the tough competition in sports makes it a good petri dish to study the complexities of strategy. He takes heart in what Albert Camus said regarding morality, '. . . everything I know most surely about morality and duty, I owe to football.' He is married to Dr Anjana Bhagyanathan, who teaches architecture at NIT Calicut. Their kids enjoy playing sports, which the author continues to try and understand.

Celebrating 35 Years of
Penguin Random House India

PRAISE FOR THE BOOK

'*Strategy Huddle* dives into the intricacies of strategy-making by captains, agents and players in a variety of sport arenas, and Deepak Dhayanithy's passionate interest in both sports and strategy has enabled him to translate these intricacies lucidly into both known and unknown strategy lessons for management—creating a must-read for both budding managers and business leaders'—Ganesh Prabhu, professor, strategy, IIM Bangalore

'*Strategy Huddle: Management Lessons from Sports* is a unique book which brings to light lessons in strategic management through the sports industry and successful sportsmen. It explains concepts in strategic management through lessons learnt from different sporting disciplines. It is a highly enjoyable read and a must-read for leaders in organizations and sports aficionados. It will also encourage business schools to offer courses on strategy from a fresh perspective as Professor Deepak has been practising at IIM Kozhikode. His passion for sports and strategy is evident in this well-researched book'—Atanu Chaudhuri, associate professor, technology and operations, Durham University Business School, and fellow, Wolfson Research Institute for Health and Wellbeing

'Deepak Dhayanithy has done a Rolf Dobelli, creating a brilliant compendium of management lessons from the world of sports. Most managers quote *Moneyball*. It was a great lesson, but the Oakland Athletics never won anything. The real leaders learn from Coach Pop, whose leadership principles built the greatest sports franchise in San Antonio. This book has that and twenty-seven other equally amazing lessons'—Avnish Anand, co-founder, CaratLane

'Everyone "knows" sports, but hardly anyone has studied them with the passion and insight that Professor Dhayanithy has. More importantly for us, he has brilliantly extracted insights from those sports and translated them to the world of business and management, using easy language that will appeal to every manager out there. Essential reading'—Sudhir Kamath, CEO and co-founder, 9stacks. com (online poker) and Faboom.com (fantasy sports), formerly MD/CEO, Suntera Energy, and consultant, McKinsey & Co.

'Sports, whether individual or the team variety, capture the popular imagination like no other. Distilling the management lessons from the lives and work of sportspeople while simultaneously making for compelling reading, however, is not an easy task. *Strategy Huddle* accomplishes that task with flair, drawing on a diverse set of examples ranging from chess to esports. It should be an enjoyable and illuminating read'—Dharmendra D., Boston marathoner, running coach and management consultant

'*Strategy Huddle* explores and exposes the ubiquitous interweaving of sports and strategy across a wide spectrum of sports categories. A surgical dissection of twenty-seven well-known instances, with a refreshingly simple outlook on each of them. Deepak's innate sense and deeply personal interest in both areas shine through. A thoroughly enjoyable read for academicians and non-academicians alike'—Kishore B.V., country head, India, Altisource Asset Management Corporation

'The West (notably the United States) has a culture of boardrooms drawing inspiration from sports managers. In India, this trend remains underdeveloped. Deepak Dhayanithy breaks the mould—bringing his deep understanding and appreciation for sports to strategic management. He is one of the pioneers of educational courses marrying the fields of strategy and sports. *Strategy Huddle* is a step in the direction of taking this to the mainstream'—Unmesh Sharma, head of institutional equities, HDFC Securities Ltd

Strategy Huddle

Management Lessons from Sports

Deepak Dhayanithy

Series Editor: Debashis Chatterjee

**PENGUIN
BUSINESS**

An imprint of Penguin Random House

PENGUIN BUSINESS

USA | Canada | UK | Ireland | Australia
New Zealand | India | South Africa | China | Singapore

Penguin Business is part of the Penguin Random House group of companies
whose addresses can be found at global.penguinrandomhouse.com

Published by Penguin Random House India Pvt. Ltd
4th Floor, Capital Tower 1, MG Road,
Gurugram 122 002, Haryana, India

First published by SAGE Publications India Pvt Ltd in 2021
Published in Penguin Business by Penguin Random House India 2023

ISBN 9780143461760

Typeset in Sabon by Manipal Technologies Limited, Manipal

www.penguin.co.in

Contents

Note by Series Editor

Dear reader,

Penguin Random House–IIM Kozhikode (IIMK) Series for New Managers brings to you *Strategy Huddle: Management Lessons from Sports* from the esteemed faculty member of IIM Kozhikode—Professor Deepak Dhayanithy. The book, as the name suggests, presents diverse strategic management concepts such as the strategic value of people, network of organizations, blue ocean strategy, disruptive innovation, etc., by exploring and analysing lessons learnt from sports.

Strategy and sports have always been analogous. The Olympic ideals of faster, higher, stronger are strategy's holy grail. The book features discussions on twenty-seven different sports phenomena across nine chapters with each chapter themed on a specific strategic management topic. Diverse sports phenomena are covered, each building up to an understanding of strategic challenges. These chapters feature a rich mix of sports including soccer, marathon, gymnastics, track and field, baseball, basketball, rowing, tennis, multi-sports competitions, golf, swimming, mixed martial arts (MMA), cricket, e-sports, chess, boxing and shooting. Written in an illustrative and a colloquial manner, each of these phenomena will help readers get a better grasp and understanding of strategic management concepts. I believe you will enjoy and benefit from understanding the organizational hierarchy through structures of moneyball and football in Chapter 2 and unravel counter-intuitive and backroom team dynamics through the accounts of individual contests like chess in Chapter 5. The author also brings your attention to the learning and behavioural dynamics quite sensitively. In Chapter 7, you will apprehend how in sports like golf every shot counts and any weakness of the mind can cost you millions of dollars. To do well, competitors need to excel at the unseen and unimagined dimension of mental models.

Strategy Huddle and the other books in the Penguin Random House–IIMK Series for New Managers aim to bridge the gap between the demands of the corporate world and quality management education. As a new manager and professional, you will be ready to face the corporate world with greater clarity and confidence after reading the books in this series.

Debashis Chatterjee
Director, IIM Kozhikode

Preface

This book draws out important strategic management lessons from detailed sports accounts. Featured are discussions of twenty-seven different sports phenomena across nine chapters, each chapter dealing with a specific strategic management topic (see Table P.1 for chapters, sports and phenomena discussed). Diverse sports phenomena are covered, each building up to an understanding of a strategic challenge. A rich mix of sports are featured in these chapters including soccer, marathon, gymnastics, track and field, baseball, basketball, rowing, tennis, multi-sports competitions, golf, swimming, MMA, cricket, e-sports, chess, boxing and shooting. Attention is also drawn to development of the nation's sporting backbone (National Collegiate Athletics Association [NCAA]), gender disparity (soccer, tennis, cricket) to raise the retirement age from 45 to 46. Between 1995 and 2006, Collina officiated in Italian Serie A games, Union of European Football Associations (UEFA) Champions League as well as Fédération Internationale de Football Association (FIFA) competitions. He won the World's Best Referee award for six consecutive years from 1998 to 2003. For a remarkable 50 per cent of his international refereeing career, he was the world's best!

A key tool that Collina and every soccer referee employs are the cards in their pocket. Yellow cards and red cards are shown to players for fouling and unsportsmanlike conduct. Cards are ubiquitous in soccer. Fans would argue endlessly about how a certain yellow-card warning or a red-card dismissal changed the game. Sometimes, referees are blamed for being trigger happy with their cards and, sometimes, for being too shy in their use. The latter leads to a game having too many violent fouls and the former leads to game outcomes determined by referee decisions. Top referees like Collina had developed the knack of when to use them, when to warn players and when to simply keep the cards in their pockets. Referees with the proven acumen to allow a soccer game to flow, but within the rules of the sport, are seen officiating the big games such as World Cup and Champions League finals.

Back in 1962, Ken Aston was the referee of a World Cup game, known since as the Battle of Santiago.

Chile, the host, played Italy in a second-round game that witnessed violent play from both sides. Armed police had to intervene twice just to finish the game. Aston dismissed players from both sides. Soccer games like this could have easily been the death knell of the 'beautiful game'. That such an unfortunate spectacle unfolded on the World Cup stage (broodje80, 2012) made it impossible for the issue of violent conduct on the soccer pitch to go unattended. If games like Battle of Santiago happened frequently, it is unlikely that soccer could have professionalized, fuelled by media and brands. Many players' career would have been cruelly cut short. These levels of violence may have even merited a 'for supervised viewing only' certification. It might have become a game that hooligans dominated rather than a game that families followed. Soccer just couldn't be the draw on television that it would go on to become.

But was there a solution back in the 1960s? What could FIFA, the world soccer administrative body, do? How could players be protected and perpetrators punished? How could soccer maintain its status as one of the most-loved sports in the world?

Though the system of cautions and dismissals were firmly in place during the 1966 World Cup in England, it had come to Aston's notice that, in the football stadium, cauldron players weren't sure that they had indeed been cautioned.

Aston realized that a card system analogous to traffic lights could work—yellow for caution and red for dismissals. Aston's wife would make the first cards—yellow and red—from construction paper, cut to a size and shape that could fit in a referee's shirt pocket.

Today, most professional games feature three or four yellow-card cautions and one in every two or three games would feature a red-card dismissal. Playing with one less player after a dismissal—that is, nine outfield players versus the opponent's ten—is a significant disadvantage in soccer. So is playing with key players under the cloud of yellow-card sanctions—one mistimed tackle could lead to their dismissal.

Professional soccer-player contracts, today, could include clauses pertaining to yellow-card cautions and red-card dismissals. Teams wouldn't want players to play at anything less than their physical and competitive best. At the same time, coaches and managers are mindful of the boundary between competitive physicality and dangerous play or violence. To a large extent, rather than Battle-of-Santiago scenarios, the worst we have today is some games/teams being littered with yellow-card cautions and red-card dismissals.

> The best referees, like Collina, work to keep the cards in their pockets, hoping that the credible threat of the cards is sufficient to maintain player discipline on the pitch.

Less experienced referees may show more cards, but over their refereeing careers, they are expected to become mature in their use of cards. Besides, referees are attuned to the use of yellow and red cards right from the start of their refereeing career. One can't be too shocked to see cards employed even in school games. These days, it is not only players who are professional; refereeing is professionalized too. The best referees would get to officiate in the biggest games. Collina's popularity was so high that he even featured in commercials like the top soccer players did.

Cards have become a target of tactical attention. Some players may fall in an exaggerated manner in order to draw the referee's attention to an egregious offense meriting a card. Some managers may instruct players to 'earn' a second yellow card and miss a relatively unimportant group game rather than risk missing important semi-finals or finals. Some players may commit cynical fouls to prevent an opponent's progress towards goal by willing to accept a yellow card.

> So, we get to witness the unseemly act of wantonly committing yellow-card offences in the pre-quarterfinal game.

So, yes—it is not a perfect system, the one driven by yellow and red cards. But is the card system a step up from the quiet, non-transparent marking in the referee's book which left players, somewhat, confused about the gravity of the warnings received? It appears so.

The solid growth of soccer in the world of sports entertainment stands testimony to the overall effectiveness of the disruptive innovation—cards. One struggles to comprehend how the worldwide telecast of soccer would have grown if there had to be a 'viewer discretion' warning going hand in hand with every telecast. In 2019, the Frenchwoman Stephanie Frappart refereed the European Super Cup game, UEFA's showpiece event between Liverpool and Chelsea (men). She led a team of women who officiated the match (lineswomen, video referees and match referees). She had also been in charge of the Women's World Cup final between the US and Netherlands as well.

> The cards were disruptive and introduced a totally new dynamic from the 1970 World Cup in Mexico when they were first implemented.

Cards have played a huge role in preserving the beautiful game. Pele signed off on an incredible World Cup career of three wins in the 1970 World Cup. Players like Pele, who brought great speed and skill to the game, thereby making it beautiful, have much to thank Aston for the card innovation! The delightfully skilful Croatian footballer, Luka Modric, changes direction on a dime, in the middle of the park, with players all around him, sprinting full steam, ball at his feet, knowing full well that were he to be stopped by an unfair challenge, card sanctions would ensue—protecting his skilful play and penalizing clumsy challenges. In hundreds and thousands of such instances, cards encourage a youngster playing with skill to ply that trade without fear of injury.

Cards are an important arsenal in the referee's hands. But they are more than that, too. In a manner that maybe Aston didn't fully anticipate or expect, the humble card contributes to the drama and beauty that unfolds on a soccer pitch.

Decades after Aston's innovation, Collina emerged and dominated the world of top-flight soccer referees due in significant part to his sophisticated understanding of this tool. In particular, he was among the small group of referees who realized that even the refrain from brandishing cards was a powerful weapon.

While many referees brandished the cards more often to maintain player discipline on the pitch, crème-de-la-crème amongst them developed, like Collina, a more sophisticated—some may even say, humane—use of cards.

Comaneci Salto

In 1976, the fourteen-year-old Romanian, Nadia Comaneci won three Olympic gold medals in gymnastics—individual overall, uneven bars and the beam. Four years later in Moscow, now a young woman, she won two gold and two silver medals. It is seldom, even in the world of sports, that what people remember the most of an athlete was accomplished at fourteen. Back then, gymnasts' routines were scored on a scale with 10 being the maximum. Scores were awarded by each of the judges on the basis of the difficulty level of the routine and the precision and flawlessness of the execution. What Comaneci achieved in Montreal was the perfect 10. The electronic score boards showed a score of 1.000 after a flawless and exhilarating performance on the uneven bars which included the 'Comaneci salto'. The scoreboards weren't calibrated to show the perfect 10! She would, in that Olympics, score a total of seven perfect 10s on the way to winning three gold medals.

She started in gymnastics very early, from pre-school. Bela Karolyi, her coach, was starting his gymnastics coaching career, from a background in boxing and hammer throw, helped by his wife, Marta, who was already a gymnastics coach. Coach and pupil were learning the intricacies of gymnastics largely through experimentation. This learning expedition was fuelled by Comaneci's dedication and willingness to put in even more effort than demanded by the coach. She would repeat routines until the perfect execution of routines had become second nature to her muscle memory. Comaneci and Karolyi were in an intense three-way competition that was pushing the boundaries of gymnastics in the 1970s. Olga Korbut of Belorussia coached by Renald Kynsh and Lyudmila Turishcheva of Russia coached by Vladislav Rastorotsky were already established when Comaneci joined them at the forefront of gymnastics.

> Gymnasts typically focus on elements of the routine which are already present in the points systems judges used to award points to a gymnastics routine. The Comaneci salto, like any departure from routines already on the points system, was hence a risk.

Like many new elements, the Comaneci salto emerged through a mistake that she'd made during practice on a traditional salto. In a traditional salto, the gymnast starts the somersault on the low bar and ends it on the high bar (of the uneven bars). Comaneci had struck her foot on the low bar. This experience gave rise to the idea of the Comaneci salto. Here, the gymnast starts and ends the straddled front somersault on the same bar.

Over more than four decades, the Comaneci salto remains an element of high-difficulty level and risk, which few gymnasts attempt in their routines.

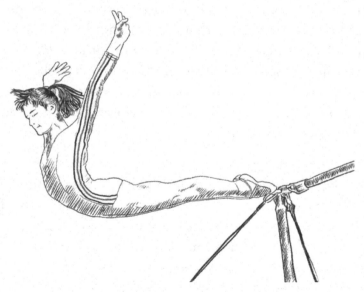

llustration 1.1: Nadia Comaneci

Four years on, at the 1980 Moscow Olympics, Comaneci had grown from a slender fourteen-year-old girl to a graceful and full-figured young woman. Her mental strength and fortitude to the fore. In a performance that is talked about much lesser than, perhaps, it ought to be, she had won two gold and two silver medals! This was in spite of multiple delays and shuffling of the time when she would start her routine and in spite of judging standards being, somewhat, malleable in Moscow towards ensuring victory for the home favourite, Yelena Davydova. Indeed, the gymnastics-points system has undergone significant changes, keeping up with the times. So, have judging standards.

Even now, forty-four years hence, those with only a fleeting familiarity with gymnastics remember Nadia Comaneci and her perfect 10. She would score nineteen perfect 10s in her career. In 1989, at the age of twenty-eight, she would defect to the US, where she would contribute to the growth of gymnastics.

Kipchoge's 1:59:40 Marathon

In 2019, the orchestrated attempt at the two-hour marathon in Vienna was a success! Water being handed to the runner, five pace-setting runners in front of and beside him, couple of runners behind him, laser guides in front of the pace-setters and a lap route in Vienna are the important reasons why this time wouldn't be an official world record (WR). The official WR for the marathon is, by the way, in Kipchoge's name as well. He had set the WR of 2:01:39 in Berlin. It was a little after his first attempt at the two-hour mark (under orchestrated settings) had failed in Monza, Italy, 2017. In Vienna, Kipchoge and his team pulled

off metronomic splits, never going outside of 2:48–
2:52 for a kilometre. With the tape in sight and the
two-hour marathon firmly in grasp, the pace setters
gradually peeled away, allowing Kipchoge to take the
tape and glory of the first-ever sub two-hour marathon,
stopping the clock at an awe-inspiring 1:59:40.

Kipchoge's race team had been based in Kenya,
training quietly in practically the same time zone as
Vienna, where the assault was planned.

> Leading up to the race day, Kipchoge had stuck to his
> simple message. He was doing this to leave behind a
> worthwhile legacy—'there were no limits to human
> achievement'.

He had, simply, picked the worthwhile challenge
that was right in front of him at the pinnacle of the
marathon. He had maintained that the knowledge
of the two-hour barrier being broken would be
significant. It would offer renewed vigour and energy
to thousands of marathoners. It would encourage the
marathon elite to go even faster, be even braver. He
had avoided getting drawn into anything that remotely
resembled spin. Why was Ineos the partner . . . ? Role
of Nike . . . ? And so on.

It is not a mean feat to reach 4:33 for each of the
26.2 miles even for Kipchoge and his pacers; forty-
two world-class distance runners in teams of seven

each rotated to pace Kipchoge around the Vienna park circuit. In competitive distance events, running splits of this nature may simply expose the runner to getting outkicked near the completion of the race. Yes, top runners glance over their shoulders and, sometimes, worry if they are going too fast!

Disruptive Innovation in Action

Scholars are in agreement about the following when it comes to the business of innovating. First, to innovate you have to change your mental model and you have to change reality (see de Brabandere & Iny, 2010). Second, it takes blood, sweat and tears. Not all innovation attempts are immediate successes or even successes at all; significant investment of time and effort go into making innovation attempts. Serendipity plays a significant role in innovation as well. Third, the best ideas would get copied by competitors; the toughest competitors would copy the best ideas effectively, hence, resting on past innovation laurels is outright dangerous. Scholars of management and strategy have likened a leader's challenge to the challenge of resetting mental models from the impossible to the possible (Taylor, 2018).

To Change We Have to Change Twice

First, we have to change our perception, our mental model. Then we have to change reality (Harkins, 2017).

Successful innovation requires imagination, great skill, organizational horsepower and leadership to achieve. Joseph A. Schumpeter (Ziemnowicz, 2013) spoke about how the gales of destruction have a strong influence on industry. Incumbents focus on their current value matrix, the current set of processes and exchanges through which they create value for customers. On the other hand, disrupters seek to set up, sometimes, entirely new value matrices. In the 1960s, a clear, specific and transparent process for disciplining a soccer game was a clear shift away from the situation when a player was simply told by the referee of his being booked (warned). What was earlier a conversation between the referee and the players became an integral event of the game—the referee brandishing his/her card. Like a team conceding a corner kick or a free kick, a player getting booked became an event in a soccer game that could strongly influence the outcome. For Kipchoge, a two-hour marathon was real in his head before plans, designs and strategies could be imagined, designed, collaborated upon and implemented.

Blood, Sweat, Tears and Serendipity

In 1976, Nadia Comaneci was a slight, petite gymnast with an enormous appetite for repeating elements, even risky ones, and routines so many times that they would come naturally to her. She had a terrific capability to shut out emotion and distractions and, simply, focus on nailing her routine. She had been a gymnast from her pre-school days. Some mistakes that she'd committed in practice had given her coach, Bela Karolyi, ideas for a new, difficult routine—Comaneci salto—which she went on to execute flawlessly, scoring 7 perfect 10s at the stage where it mattered—1976 Montreal Olympics. With relentless practice, a child's body and mind all came together in a manner difficult to emulate. Indeed, rule changes mean that somebody aged fourteen wouldn't even be allowed to compete these days.

Something as boring and unremarkable as hundreds of repetitions at the gym play a big role in the perfect 10. It takes even greats like Kipchoge and the phalanx of supporting organizations and runners two attempts (Monza 1917 and Vienna 1919) to reach their goal. Nadia Comaneci's perfect 10 involved only a small, tiny fraction of capital and technologies in comparison to Kipchoge's sub two-hour marathon, but let us not forget that it was in Romania, then, behind the iron curtain.

Nothing Lasts Forever

History is testimony to the psychological gravitas of barriers such as the perfect 10 in gymnastics or the two-hour marathon. Once one athlete shows that it can be done, others follow. In the years since the first perfect 10 was executed, other gymnasts have

emulated the feat. That is the hope of Kipchoge's
1:59:40. It is quite likely that one of the forty-two
distance runners who helped him to the mark may
themselves further improve the time. Maybe, they will
do it under official marathon conditions, creating a
sub-two WR! Disruptive innovators need to continue
with sustaining innovations in order to retain their lead.
Or better still, make the next big splash themselves.
The smartphone market wasn't won once and for all
with the successful launch of the iPhone. It merely
reintroduced the company, Apple, to the world as a
product leader. Retaining that place of pre-eminence
is more like a sub two-hour marathon assault. As
kilometre after kilometre passes, the required pace
may slip. In Kipchoge's first attempt, this slipping was
barely perceptible at first. But it gained momentum.
In the end, the assault failed by 25 seconds. At world-
class marathon pace, that's about 100 metres behind
where one needs to be. Margins between glory and
failure are razor thin.

Disruptive Innovation in Other Businesses

Just as Ken Aston, back in the 1960s, could think of
a fresh, transparent way of ensuring the discipline in a
game of soccer or just how Kipchoge could imagine the
two-hour marathon, innovators across industries are
able to look beyond the here and now. They are able to
conceive their business in entirely new and fresh ways.

Online Management Education at IIMK

In the face of scepticism, it takes someone to say, 'Yes, we will have online classrooms.' Somebody said that and built a successful online MBA program at IIMK way back in 2008 (IIMK, 2020). Slowly, but surely, massive open online courses and live internet classrooms as well as live internet tutors emerged. By 2020, during the Covid-19 pandemic, live internet classrooms had become ubiquitous not just in executive and postgraduate education but even in undergraduate colleges and schools. While the sheer technological capability to drive the current remote classrooms have emerged over the past two decades, IIMK had conceptualized and launched remote, executive classes over a decade and a half ago. The pandemic served to provide the impetus required to take the classroom to pretty much any corner of the country that has a good internet connection.

Apple's Resurrection with iPhone

Just as the sheer persistence of Nadia Comaneci back in Romania as a teenager or Kipchoge's in his pursuit of the two-hour marathon, innovators endure blood, sweat and tears. They are able to dig deep under adversity. Richard Rumelt (Lovallo & Mendonca, 2007), strategy scholar par excellence, says this about how Apple returned to its place of pre-eminence under

Steve Jobs with its iPod and iPhones. As different parts of the Apple design and engineering divisions got close to breakthrough products, the organization itself teetered on the precipice of delinquency in 2000–01. Rumelt, on account of working closely with Steve Jobs, had a ringside seat to the drama as it unfolded. Steve Jobs managed to create an atmosphere within which the design and engineering horsepower of Apple could succeed. Alan Turing, the spiritual guru of Apple, endured many difficulties keeping faith in the promise of the Turing machine, during the Second World War (WWII). Just as well, that persistence may have won WWII for the Allies. Strategy and innovation may be as simple as that for some organizations—keep the wheels turning and recognize the magic when it happens.

Mobile Computing

Just as how Kipchoge expects his sub-two-hour marathon to drive fellow marathoners to greater heights, various other industries have benefited enormously once the path had been shown. Consider Moore's law and Hwang's law. Once scientific minds established that computing power could be crammed into smaller and smaller devices, the capability of computers and smartphones skyrocketed. Showing the way is only the start of the challenge. Companies like Intel and Samsung electronics (Siegel & Chang,

2005) have proven to be adept at continually driving up the capabilities of their devices and technologies. First hurdle is to instil organizational faith in the continued growth of computing power. Second is the implementation or innovation challenge of pulling off better memory products, quarter after quarter, so that the promise can be realized.

Be it in the highest echelons of sport or the highest echelons of technology-driven businesses, disruptive innovation is the biggest challenge. Clayton Christensen's principles are played out by athletics teams and business organizations. Both groups would rather be disruptive innovators than witness their ways getting disrupted unexpectedly by other competitors.

2

Internal Organization and Winning Core Competencies

'If we think like them in here, we'll lose to 'em out there . . .' (Billy Beane, played by Brad Pitt, extols in the movie *Moneyball*)

Strategy is about winning, not whining—about the capital constraints or a tough business or the pain of a visionary. Be it the Oakland Athletics (baseball) or TSG Hoffenheim or Liverpool Football Club (both soccer), the key lies in understanding how to win with what we have. This leads, often, to recognizing resources and capabilities that everyone else missed, just as the strategies of Southwest Airlines or Starbucks or, indeed, Indigo (Chen & Garg, 2018). C.K. Prahalad's concept of 'core competencies' holds the valuable key to the answer.

America's Favourite Pastime and Moneyball

In 1971, the Society for American Baseball Research was founded and lent its name to sabermetrics—the application of statistics to various in-game actions and events, to answer questions critical to the understanding of performance in baseball. Baseball is to America what cricket is to India. The MLB (Major League Baseball) is to America what the Indian Premier League (IPL) is to India, just a lot more than it appears. MLB comprises thirty franchise teams (IPL has eight) which play 162 games each (IPL has fourteen) during the regular season. Then there are the playoffs culminating in best-of-seven finals playoff. A total of 2430 regular season games are played in one MLB year (IPL has fifty-six).

> Although a team game, just like cricket, baseball is dominated by individual matchups, contests and events.

Since recording of these events in the scoreboards and newspaper box scores is ubiquitous, pioneers like Bill James were able to examine the importance of each of these events in the larger context of the game. Deep dive into these dynamics led to important measurements in a world where player costs represented 60–80 per cent of the costs to an MLB franchise. Investments in player scouting, hiring and development needed to be

managerial and leadership gumption of Billy Beane to get the job done.

But there was more to it than only sabermetrics.

Sandy Anderson, who Billy Beane succeeded as the Oakland Athletics GM, had voiced these sabermetric ideas. However, that was a time when the team owners had adequate capital and the appetite to splurge on star players whose valuations were sky high.

> Billy Beane's career as GM had a different context. He himself had flamed out after having been a highly anticipated college star. This personal experience found a strong reference in Bill James' work and fuelled his passion to drive real performance in baseball—his passion to not be fooled by the odd, extraordinary events which many fans may cling on to!

Power hits that cleared the stadium once in a while was good to have. But what was better was someone who got on base consistently.

A shortstop with great athletic ability was good to have. What was better was a shortstop whose anticipation and shifting on weight helped him stop more hits in the infield itself.

> Profiles of MLB owners were also changing. MLB team owners were increasingly people from the world of business and investments.

To them, player valuations driven by their contribution to team success (wins) was intuitive. Further, team owners like John Henry, of the Boston Red Sox, were comfortable with numbers and could appreciate what Bill James had started more than fifty years ago. So much so that John Henry looked at Billy Beane as the sort of GM who could lead the Red Sox to the elusive World title. Henry looked at Billy Beane as the sort of GM who could help the Red Sox break the 'curse of the Bambino'—they hadn't won the World title since their 1914 sale of Babe Ruth to the arch-rival, New York Yankees.

Once the MLB World title was won, it was time to look across the pond.

Total Football—Barcajax

New England Sports Ventures (NESV), owned jointly by John Henry, Tom Werner, Les Otten, the New York Times Company and other investors, also bought majority stake in Liverpool Football Club in 2010. However, soccer (football) is very different from baseball. It is not a game defined by separate, one-on-one contests! Soccer is a very fluid game that, for a long time, had defied statistical analysis.

> Way back in 1965, on taking over as manager of Ajax Football Club, Rinus Michels put to work a playing style which is now referred to as 'total football'.

While total football has many source teams, coaches and clubs, its most accepted wellspring has Rinus Michels as the guru and Johan Cruyff as its prime locomotor. Total football ideas were implemented thoroughly in the Dutch national football team of 1974 and Ajax teams of that era—1971 onwards.

> The idea was simple. Every outfield player was comfortable playing every position, and therefore, the team would feature a fluid interchange of playing position depending on situation of the game.

Defenders could attack, forwards could defend, central midfielders could operate on the flanks and so on. Total football was an aesthetically pleasing alternative to rigid structures which assigned players to each of the positions on the soccer pitch. In order to glide up and down the field and across it, players needed to have a high degree of skill and trust in each other. Squads needed to be comprised of more skilful players who understood this system and could change positions intelligently and effortlessly. Defenders making deep runs into enemy territory were comforted in the knowledge that the gap they left behind would not remain open for long. Other players would rotate and the gap would be gone before the opponent could exploit it. This dynamic adjustment of every player to everything that is going on around him/her is called 'strategic endogenous response' (SER).

SER is a key feature of soccer, the soul of the beautiful game. It was taken to its extreme in total football. In order for teams to achieve success playing this brand of soccer, players needed to have a high level of spatial intelligence in addition to skill and trust.

> Spatial intelligence helps players comprehend relative position and its evolution over time not only of themselves but the ball, their teammates and opponents as well.

Around the same time, in the early 1970s, on one side of the Atlantic, the individual matchups and events-driven sport of baseball was being revolutionized by sabermetrics, whereas on the other side of the pond, the fluid sport of soccer was being revolutionized by the spatial dynamism of total football. Netherlands may have lost the 1974 World Cup final to West Germany, but they had already won many hearts and minds. Ajax and Dutch teams of the generation left their opponent awestruck. Johann Cruyff, a native of Amsterdam, captained many of those teams.

> When Cruyff played for the Spanish club, Futbol Club Barcelona (FCB) for five seasons from 1973 to 1978, he took total football ideas with him.

More importantly, perhaps, the captain dragged what was a despondent Catalan club and turned in worthy, on-field performances. After fourteen long years, FCB won the La Liga league title in 1974 and gave a good account of itself in European soccer competitions. In 1985, Cruyff started his managerial career in Ajax. He would arrive in Barcelona in 1988–89, having gained experience in implementing total football ideas at Ajax (where Rinus Michels had implemented these ideas as a coach, way back in 1974). A decade on from when he was an FCB player, Cruyff, the manager, implemented ideas that have since been referred as 'barcajax'—reference to the club where it all started, Ajax and FCB, the club where top talents plied total football relentlessly.

Cruyff assembled a squad featuring top international-player talent. His teams included Pep Guardiola (Spain), Histov Stoichkov (Bulgaria), Ronald Koeman (Netherlands) and Gheorghe Hagi (Romania). In the five seasons between 1989 and 1994, FCB won the Spanish league four times and the European Cup (today's Champions League) in 1992.

Playing squads were to be constructed keeping in mind the philosophy of total football. Yes, winning games and championships were just as important as they are to any sporting organization. Barcajax demanded more. The team's play needed to be aesthetically pleasing as well.

As manager for the first team, Cruyff demanded these skills and sensibilities from the FCB pipeline of youth talent.

> He had seen that developing a squad with the cohesion, spatial intelligence, skill and trust went well beyond training players as professionals.

In the early 1990s, the new youth training facility was built and became the youth development home, La Masia. More than two decades on from when Cruyff took over as manager at FCB, in the 2010 World Cup, Spain won the World Cup in South Africa, shedding their 'also ran' tag. Couple of years later, they won the European national competition as well.

So, what has Spain's performances in the 2010s got to do with total football or Ajax or Cruyff or Barcelona? Fair question.

The seven players who started for Spain in that 2010 World Cup final in Johannesburg against the Netherlands came through La Masia and plied their trade professionally for Barcelona—Carles Puyol (centre back), Gerard Piqué (centre back), Segio Busquets (defensive midfielder), Xavi (attacking midfield), Andrés Iniesta (attacking midfield), Pedro (winger) and Villa (striker). Cesc Fàbregas, who also played for Barcelona, came on as a substitute. So, what is the big deal? Let's see.

In the 1990s, they were kids in the La Masia which Cruyff helped build. Xavi joined La Masia when he was eleven. Iniesta was older—fifteen—when he joined. Victor Valdez, the substitute goalkeeper; Xavi Hernandez, the puppet master; and Gerard Piqué, the centre back, were only ten years old when they came to La Masia. Carles Puyol, Piqué's central defensive partner at the 2010 World Cup, and Sergio Busquets, the defensive midfielder, were older—seventeen. At La Masia (the farmhouse), kids with the potential footballing talent were trained in football, attended school and grew up playing football together.

An important characteristic that La Masia look for in its potential students was, in addition to the footballing skill and talent, humility and an unassuming nature. This may not jump out as a particularly important trait especially at a time when aggression and being outspoken are seen as positives for professional sportsmen and sportswomen.

Right from the Cruyff days, the belief was instilled in La Masia that a 'humble' person would be more open to learning new things. A better learner would be able to adapt and improve over time. And, in a hyper-competitive world, what mattered was the ability to keep improving.

This generation would go on to win great laurels for themselves individually, for the clubs they played professionally in, and for Spain in World Cup and European National competitions. Cruyff died in 2016 at the age of sixty-eight. Lollipops were left at the feet of the photographs and flowers—by Cules, Catalans, FCB fans and soccer fans—in his homage. Following years of being a heavy smoker, he had taken to lollipops on the touchline as manager.

> Though Cruyff has passed away, total football lives on. No modern goalkeeper features on a team sheet unless he or she can also play as a sweeper back, assured with the ball at their feet.

In the 2014 World Cup, Oliver Kahn, the German goalkeeper, completed more passes than Lionel Messi, the Argentinian forward. Pep Guardiola was a player Cruyff promoted into the first team ranks. Pep was at the helm when the World Cup winning generation were given a go in the FCB system.

Cruyff took the route of identifying and developing players with the skills, attitudes, humility and spatial intelligence to succeed with total football. That route made sense in the context of the beautiful game. Reporting and tracking of the game hadn't, even in the 1990s, reached a level where sabermetric approaches could succeed. That route didn't start with the starting squads he coached at Barcelona. It went deeper. At La Masia, the selected kids were presented with the unique opportunity to excel in Barcelona colours while, at the same time, taking in a world class school education. Some of those kids would go on to win laurels that made it impossible for professional soccer to not inculcate total football principles into the way they competed.

Moneyball Crosses the Atlantic

By the 2000s (Lewis, 2003), clubs like TSG Hoffenheim now had access to spatial technology tools which allowed them to develop a style of playing that was sophisticated enough to upend more established teams, on larger budgets, competing in an archaic manner. Between 2006 and 2008, TSG Hoffenheim went from being in one of the lower rungs to the top division—Bundesliga—in Germany. Footbonauts used in training were useful in inculcating precise player movement skills, ones that could be internalized through countless hours of practice. By that time, in professional games, players wore tracking devices on their shirts which recorded every move of every player, every fraction of a second. After a match, the coach could show players what was going on spatially, 'eye in the sky', so to speak. Player training thereby became that much more efficient.

NESV owned jointly by John Henry, Tom Werner, Les Otten, the New York Times Company and other

point services; employees who could fulfil alternative duties were the key.

Southwest established an attractive fit between frequent departures, point-to-point services and simple, walk-up ticketing. Frequent departures and simple, walk-up ticketing—this combination saved costs and addressed the needs of the budget and business flyer. Frequent departures and point-to-point services were, again, tightly coupled with one another. This satisfied customer service at the low-price point where it could dominate the market. Once businesses are able to develop process and capabilities around their VRIN resources, they are in a position to develop and leverage core competencies. Core competencies allow firms to gain access to multiple product and factor markets. In each of these markets, they may not rely on the same product configuration with which they had won in their business originally.

Starbucks

Fit is of utmost importance when it comes to winning at the business of a low-cost airline or high-quality coffee experience, as well. For Starbucks to succeed in its vision of being the third place, home and work being the other two, being within a ten-minute walk from one's office is the key. This made store real estate on the edge and corners of busy office precincts very valuable. Throughout its history of stellar growth,

Starbucks' real estate teams kept in touch with the quality and quantity of store real estate in the market. This allowed them to move fast when it came to opening new stores in prime Starbucks real estate. By its very nature, this real estate was valuable, rare, inimitable as well as non-substitutable! Interestingly, this careful attention to real estate locations was a core driver of the growth of McDonald's as well.

For Starbucks, well-trained baristas fit with the great locations of stores as well as coffee makers inbuilt with the settings on the roasting curves. Well-trained baristas, great locations and high-quality coffee makers all come only with consistent investment over a relatively long period of time. This combination ensured that Starbucks was able to attract its clientele to stores where their coffee experience is of a high quality.

Indigo

When flying in India, it is quite common to see the Indigo (and other low-cost airlines') staff at the check-in counter also collect boarding passes and usher passengers from security to the aircraft. Developing core competencies helps organizations access multiple-product markets. For example, Starbucks in India has upmarket location footprint, mainly. Their finely-tuned, high-quality coffee experience allows this leeway. Airlines like Indigo have, relatively, quickly started offering international connections and have built out an impressively young fleet of aircraft. Their attention to detail pertaining to cost reduction has helped them access these other opportunities.

Being able to discern VRIN resources and capabilities, building out organizations on its basis—that is long, hard work where organizations often look up to a strategist to show the way. In an environment that is always in flux, the internal resolve to do things a certain way—to look for a certain type of battling mentality, or a certain sort of spatial intelligence—is quite difficult. Be it Starbucks or Southwest or Indigo or sports organizations like Oakland A's, barcajax, TSG Hoffenheim or, indeed, Liverpool, this focus on strengthening the organization can pay handsome dividends as well!

3

Appreciating the External Environment

A beautiful countryside, a river, a growing socialite class, universities growing in stature and a rowing rivalry sponsored by a railway company was born. Seeds of the NCAA were sown, and the US college sport would go on to play an influential role in the development of sporting dreams, national and international, for men and women. How businesses slot themselves in their environment, deriving strength from their surroundings and from national ethos, is fascinating. Porter's models are highly influential, and somebody figured it out just thinking about a rowing race back in 1852! Just examine Uber, Audi or Byju's to understand the strength of this approach to strategy.

'Given encouragement and ample opportunity, female students become interested in athletic programs,' the report said. 'They practise seriously and strenuously. Given ample support and publicity, women's sports can create as much spectator interest as men's sports.'

An article that appeared in a 1969 *Sports Illustrated* observed, 'Many of the girls, born into farm families, grow up well conditioned for basketball's physical demands. (But) At the time, women's college sport was significantly under-invested.'

Women's sports budget was less than a twelfth of the budget for men's sports.

Men's teams travelled on chartered buses for their away games, whereas collegiate sportswomen were left to fend for themselves to fund travel, practice and other costs. When given the opportunities and the means, women became more interested in sports, just like the men. Across many sports, there has since been a strong increase in the opportunities for women to participate. In soccer, for instance, there were twenty-two collegiate teams in Division 1, NCAA sponsored, competition in 1980. By 2018–19, there were 333—a fifteen-fold increase!

> Over this time, the US had emerged as a powerhouse
> in women's soccer. The Stars and Stripes won the
> Women's World Cup in 1991, 1999, 2015 and 2019.
> They finished runners-up in 2011.

The seeds of this success were sowed way back
with Title IX. In 1971, there were only 700 female,
high-school soccer players and, by 2019, there were
390,481—a growth factor of 558! Mia Hamm and
Hope Solo have become household names of the
beautiful game. Christie Rampone was part of the
US women's triumphs at the World Cup in 1999 and
2015, praised by a commentator for, amongst other
things, being a 'world-class human being'.

National Collegiate Athletics Association

Of about 8 million US high school students who
compete in sports, about one in sixteen would make to
be collegiate sportsmen and sportswomen. Of the less
than half a million NCAA athletes, only a select few
would make it to the professional leagues. That said,
the NCAA, which organizes intercollegiate sports in
the US, gives the chance and platform for thousands
and thousands of young, aspiring sports people.
Athletic scholarships of over $3.5 billion, annually,
were awarded. Sports stars are typically identified

in this developmental, college stage itself. Brands, coaches, athletic directors, etc., exert great influence in this 'amateur' environment. Its history is a long one and started with a boat race back in the 19th century.

In the 1840s, universities were being set up all over the US. Harvard and Yale were already well-established universities, attracting top academic talent. They each had established rowing clubs as well. American football and basketball were yet to be invented. Back then, rowing was the most popular recreational activity in the US. According to Bill Miller, 'It didn't take long for someone to suggest that . . . Harvard and Yale . . . agree to a race' (Shiff, 2017). The Boston, Concord and Montreal Railroad (BCMR) sponsored the regatta as promotion for their excursion trains. Along the length of the River Thames in New London, where the race was held, these excursion train cars with flat tops allowed spectators to watch and follow the race from start to finish (Harvard, 2002).

The Harvard–Yale regatta developed into a major sporting and social event, even attracting heavy betting. In 1925, there were an estimated 100,000 spectators. 'Special 32-car observation trains with grandstands atop flatcars rolled along the riverbank to follow the crews.'

Illustration 3.1: Harvard–Yale Crew Races Sponsored by BCMR

The first student athletes, the rowers or crew at Harvard and Yale, needed to be exemplary students as well as exemplary rowers to gain admission into these universities. This rivalry '. . . took hold in collegiate athletic culture just as colleges were being established all over the nation and collegiate sports were beginning to evolve.' Balancing the demands of being a collegiate oarsman with the academic demands of Harvard and Yale required the individual to be driven to succeed.

Given the vibrant college athletics environment, college sport gave rise to a number of marketable brands and sports personalities. Sponsorship spending on college athletics was over $1.2 billion in the 2017–18 season (College Sports, 2018). Insurance, automotive, banks, retail, quick service restaurant, sports apparel, telecom, soft drink, medical, ticketing, fuel, logistics and airlines sectors were all represented when it came to brands' sponsorships of the college game in 2017–18

(Janoff, 2018). In 2019, NCAA revenues were $1.118 billion. More than 80 per cent of that came from fees for television and marketing rights (NCAA, 2018–19). NCAA distributed these revenues to its member colleges based on their division and invested in association-wide programs. For a median Division I school, NCAA distributions in 2013 were over $10 million and that was almost 17 per cent of the athletic departmental revenues (Covell & Walker, 2013). Ticket sales, alumni donations, royalties and fees contributed 34 per cent of the revenues for the athletic department. The median university spend on athletic scholarships was about $9 million in 2013.

Athletic scholarships attracted the best high school talent. Individual athletes could have various considerations as well—education and campus experience, opportunity to play in strong sides, opportunity to play under a great coach and so on.

Tim Duncan, San Antonio Spurs star, studied in Wake Forest University from 1993 to 1997 and, on graduation, was drafted by the Spurs. Over the four years, he garnered a number of individual player honours under coach Dave Odom, drawing NBA interest.

Duncan's college career is not the norm though. Many student athletes tend to struggle academically.

With only 2 per cent of college athletes going pro, educational attainment of student athletes assumes added significance. Misconduct and law breaking of student athletes, university boosters attracting high school talent with financial inducements are the most serious challenges facing the NCAA.

College sport is a spectacle in and of itself. NCAA television contracts with top television broadcasters stand testimony to this. These multi-billion-dollar contracts have a value of over $1 billion, annually, for NCAA. University of Texas, a top earning athletic department, belongs to the Big-12 conference and had total annual revenues of over $200 million in 2018. Tenth on the list was Florida University, part of the Southeastern Conference (SEC), which earned $161 million.

In the US intercollegiate sports, conferences create local rivalries which stoke interest in athletic competition. The conference also helps minimize squad travel for away games. Intra- and extra-conference rivalries are a big part of what makes college sport tick commercially.

The largest conference—Atlantic Coast Conference (ACC)—comprises fifteen universities whereas smaller conferences like the Ivy League comprises only eight universities.

Duke–North Carolina is one such storied college basketball rivalry (ACC). Since 1953, Duke and North Carolina have won or shared close to 80 per cent of the regular season titles and close to 60 per cent of the conference tournament titles. 137 NBA players are alumnus of either Duke or North Carolina.

Each university is faced with the problem of how to balance its athletic and academic commitments.

On one end of the spectrum are large universities that provide full athletic scholarships (Rittenberg, 2014) and attract top talent especially for the big team games. On the other end are relatively small enrolment Ivy League universities that do not provide athletic scholarships and who pride themselves of upholding the true amateur spirit of college sports. Ivy League universities compete in the confidence that their superior academic track record would draw athletes even without the athletic scholarship. Each of these types of universities draws its own sponsorship streams.

Jeremy Lin joined Harvard University which didn't offer a scholarship as Ivy League policy. After a consistently strong college career at Harvard, Lin entered the 2010 draft, not as one of the stars. He, eventually, made his mark at the big market NBA franchise, New York Knicks.

Sports coaches are some of the highest-paid university employees. The highest paid sports coaches are paid even more than the highest-paid professors in academia. Dabo Swinney, the tenth-highest-paid sports coach, earns $6.2 million a year. David N. Silvers, the Professor of Columbia University's Medical Centre, earns $4.33 million a year; Dean Takahashi, the professor of finance at Yale, earns $2.6 million and the Dean of Harvard Business School earns a little less than $1 million a year (Baron, 2015).

Katey Stone, all-time most successful college coach in women's ice hockey at Harvard and Duke University's men's basketball coach, and Mike Krzyzewski have important similarities and contrasts. Both coaches led their universities admirably for many seasons. Both contributed to national successes in their respective sport.

But Katey Stone works in a non-athletic scholarship environment and attracts athletes with academic quality, whereas Coach K runs a large athletic scholarship-driven university basketball system.

International Student Athlete's External Environment

A focal NCAA student athlete faces intense competition, day in and day out. This experience is widely believed to prepare her/him for a career in professional sports. Over the years, NCAA athletics and the US college education has attracted high-quality talent from all over the world. Just as a good number of engineering and science graduates from Indian universities seek a master's education in the US, talented sportsmen and sportswomen from all over the world have sought to pursue bachelor's education and their sporting ambitions in US colleges. Only 5 per cent of high school athletes gain entry into NCAA athletics sports programs. Only 2 per cent of college sportsmen and sportswomen make it into professional sport. What motivates athletes to pursue college sports against such odds? What motivated Suriname swimmer Anthony Nesty, Indian tennis player Mahesh Bhupathi and Swedish golfer Madelene Sagström to pursue their sports dreams via US collegiate education?

Anthony Conrad Nesty, Mahesh Bhupathi and Magdalene Sagström

In the 1984 Los Angeles Olympics, swimming for Suriname, seventeen-year-old Nesty failed to make the finals, finishing twenty-first overall in the 100 m butterfly. He had, however, done enough to gain entry to the Bolles School in Jacksonville, Florida. Founded in 1933, this prep school is reputed for imparting training to 'elite, world-class swimmers'. At Bolles, Nesty was under the tutelage of Gregg Troy, who would go on to become a storied swimming head coach of Florida University team, the Gators (ISHOF, 2020). In the 1988 Seoul Summer Olympics, Nesty won gold in the 100 m butterfly.

After his Olympic triumph, he would take up the athletic scholarship offered by Florida University. He would go on to win many laurels for the Gators, swimming in the NCAA. When his competitive swimming career came to a close, he took up coaching opportunities at his alma maters. From the mid-1990s, he coached at the Bolles School. Nesty grew through the coaching ranks and, in 2018, was made head coach of the Florida University (Gators) men's swimming teams. Nesty's career in a fine example of how he found himself in an environment which was attractive and supportive, helping him succeed.

Mahesh Bhupathi's development in tennis took a successful trajectory when this recognized Indian tennis talent joined the University of Mississippi and played for them for two years—1994 and 1995. Over these two seasons, Bhupathi won SEC titles in singles as well as the NCAA National title in doubles. At the age of twenty-one, he turned professional. He made his mark on the world stage in doubles and mixed-doubles as well as Olympics. He has won doubles titles at the French Open, Wimbledon and the US Open, while winning each of the Grand Slam events twice in mixed doubles.

Speaking to business school students in 2019–20, Bhupathi pointed to his development as a tennis player in the University of Mississippi, Ole Miss, and reflected on the world of opportunities that opened up for him being part of a formal, systematic, 'top-down' approach. The Mahesh Bhupathi Tennis Academy (MBTA) was founded in 2006 and it works towards 'imparting professional, world-class training (both practical and theoretical) and highly specialized coaching to youngsters of all age-groups' (MBTA, 2015). Today MBTA has over twenty centres across India, with 8000 children playing tennis in them. At the helm of MBTA are people with a combination of tennis and sports management experience from across the world. Bhupathi's business ventures include Globosports (Pal, 2019; celebrity brand management) and Scentials Beauty Care and Wellness Pvt Ltd (beauty products; Chaudhary, 2019).

Born in 1992, Madelene Maria Sagström joined Louisiana State University (LSU) in 2011, drawn to this Division I SEC school by the opportunity to work on her innate golf talent. Back home in Sweden, still in her teens, she was ranked twelfth in the ladies rankings. She had already found a place in the Swedish national team as well. In LSU, she earned the reputation of a strong work ethic and her average round scores improved steadily from 73.6 in her freshman year to 71.5 in her senior year (2014–15). In her junior season (third year) in 2013–14, she broke through to win her first collegiate event posting rounds scores of 70–70–66 in a field of seventy-eight golfers (Isusports, 2015).

She finished over forty golf tournaments in her college career—great preparation ground for the professional career that would follow. She went from scoring par or better in 41 per cent of the rounds in her freshman year to scoring par or better in 70 per cent of the rounds in her senior year (see Table 3.2). Now, that is a young woman taking a decisive step into the professional game!

Table 3.2 Magdelene Sagström: LSU statistics

SEASON	ROUNDS	STROKES	AVG.	PAR OR UNDER	LOW 18	LOW 54	TOP 10	BEST
2011-12	34	2,501	73.56	14	68	209	4	3
2012-13	29	2,134	73.59	12	67	213	4	2
2013-14	29	2,125	73.28	14	66	206	2	1
2014-15	33	2,359	71.48	23	67	207	8	2
Totals	125	9,119	72.95	63	66	206	18	1

Till April 2020 in the Ladies Professional Golf Association (LPGA) Tour, Sagström continued her impressive learning and performance curve. With a world ranking of fifty-one and career LPGA earning of over $1.1 million, her seven top-ten finishes and one Tour event victory should come as no surprise.

Strategic Analysis of External Environment

It is important for the strategist to take due cognizance of the EE. In the 1960s, strategists like Professor Michael Porter (Magretta, 2011) emerged from industrial organization (IO), setting out to explain why some firms succeeded consistently whereas others faltered and even failed. Examining the EE carefully has yielded answers to some key parts of this puzzle. Understanding EE can ground the strategist's contextual understanding. General EE analysis is useful to develop a broad panoramic view of dynamics which influence competitiveness. Political, economic, social, technological, environmental and legal (PESTEL; Yüksel, 2012) forces shape and reshape the business landscape, continuously. The National Diamond model—consisting of factors of production, demand conditions, firm rivalry and related industries—helps us understand this national EE. Government influence and chance also play crucial roles in this National Diamond. The EE with, perhaps, the most direct influence on a firm's strategy is its competitive context. It places firm rivalry within the context of the bargaining power of suppliers and buyers with respect to the focal firm, barriers to entry and the threat of substitution of the firm's offerings. This competitive context plays a significant role in the development of individual firms and is, perhaps, the easiest strategic management framework to recall—the Five Forces model.

External Environment in Action

In this section, we'll examine Title IX, NCAA and three International NCAA student athletes employing the

PESTEL, National Diamond and Five Forces models, respectively.

Title IX and Pestel

Although sociological (S) and political (P) upheavals were afoot in the US, especially through the 1960s, a significant win for the cause of equal opportunities for women played itself out through the law (L). Prior to the passing of Title IX into law, as part of Educational Amendment Act of 1972, women had fewer opportunities in sports. Only a miniscule percentage of sports budgets were for women's sports. Title IX affirmed that, 'No person in the United States shall, on the basis of sex, be excluded from participation in, be denied the benefits of, or be subjected to discrimination under any education program or activity receiving Federal financial assistance.' Feminist groups, more than sixty of them, played a stellar role in ensuring that Title IX didn't lose any of its legal teeth when it came to its passing into law.

Remarkably, sports participation and funding numbers that were lopsided against women began to change dramatically as well. Prior to Title IX, at the most crucial juncture of a young athlete's development—late teens, sports opportunities for women dried up. Obviously, this led to fewer young women taking up sports seriously. In turn, this created pernicious incentives for under-investment in women's sport. By 2020, female athletes were leading male athletes when it comes to admission into the US universities and scholarships. Early signs that women's sport is just as exciting (if not more) and marketable as men's sport had emerged from places like Iowa high school basketball. Here, crowds would disperse when the girls' games concluded, and the boys played in front of empty rafters. The US women's soccer team, for instance, is a world beater, featuring some of the best players and coaches in the game. Title IX's influence is clear to see.

NCAA and National Diamond

Governing sports at the US collegiate level, the NCAA has managed to successfully pull together factors (student athletes, coaches), demand (college sports arenas, television, brands), firm rivalry (high-quality, inter-university sports competitions) and related and supporting industries (sponsors, advertisers, professional league drafts). Needless to say, NCAA wields enormous power. While student athletes are amateur, NCAA sports is a huge money spinner. College athletic revenue streams include tickets, in-arena sponsors, broadcasting deals and sponsorships for sports apparel. Right from the Harvard–Yale boat race back in 1852, inter-college sports has been tightly knit together with the social milieu and as an independent profit centre within the university. Alumni donations are an important source of money for athletic departments. Back in the nineteenth century, BCMR sponsored the Harvard–Yale regatta as promotion for their excursion trains. During the regatta, more than 100,000 spectators took part in the competition along the River Thames in New England. The regatta was an important part of the summer social circle in the north-eastern US. Aspects of alumni interest and pride dovetailed into commercial opportunities; these remain an integral part of US college sport even today.

NCAA Conferences play a significant role. Local, derby-like rivalries dominate conference's regular season games. This provides adequate, regular competition which aids in the development of sportswomen and men into professionals. Over time, some conferences have become synonymous with high-quality, athletic competition. So, athletes succeeding in their chosen sport and collegiate conferences signal their high quality to professional franchises. NCAA and college campuses dominate supply of rookies to the North American professional leagues. Just one such league, National Football League, boasts revenues of more than $15 billion a year!

Not just for professional sports leagues and their franchise teams, NCAA is a developing ground for international Olympic athletes as well. For instance, the crew teams of Yale and Harvard, today feature not just the most-promising rowers of the US. Young German, English, Kiwi rowers seek to row in the NCAA competitions as well. A successful NCAA career is a good way for a talented teenager to be firmly in the reckoning for higher laurels after his or her graduation.

These create a strong network of demand, factors related and supporting industries and rivalry. The intense competition (rivalry) is the best way for a freshman (factor) to develop into a high-quality rookie courted by professional teams (demand). A more direct demand is, simply, of exciting intercollegiate competitions followed by the college faithful. Related and supporting industries like the BCMR of the mid-nineteenth century are today's Nike, Reebok and Adidas. Head coaches of team sports of Division 1 teams, like basketball Coach K of Duke, have a demigod status, often earning much higher than the respective university's presidents. Experienced coaches are the main draw for very-talented athletes to join a particular university as well. While the NCAA is not without its critics and design lacunae, its role in the successes of many individuals and teams like the all-conquering Stars and Stripes, the US women's soccer team, is obvious.

International NCAA Student Athletes and Five Forces

The international NCAA student athlete has an EE characterized by professional sports franchises that would pick only the best college talent (bargaining power to buyers is high), by NCAA scholarship offering universities that would select only the best into their programmes (bargaining power of suppliers is high), by new freshman competitors every year (low barriers to entry), by professional franchises discovering new talent pools like international basketball and baseball players (threat of substitution) and by very tough intra-conference and national competition under intense scrutiny (intensive rivalry).

For Anthony Nesty, a twenty-first-place finish in the Los Angeles Olympics was the ticket to a preparatory school, Bolles, where he came under the tutelage of great coaches and the rigorous competition. For Mahesh Bhupathi, two successful seasons at Ole Miss—conference and national winner—vaulted him to going professional. For Sagström, improving by two strokes over the four seasons at LSU put her on the way to the LPGA. Each of the above is an example of how the intensive intra- and inter-conference rivalry, regular week-in and week-out competition and access to high-value coaching inputs helped international sportsmen and sportswomen to succeed.

The IO origins of modern strategy scholarship of the 1960s focused on important, big, irreversible firm decisions as the bulwark of the discipline. When an international sportswoman makes her way to study college in the US, at the age of eighteen, her situation has strong similarities to how strategic examination of the EE started. Young, international athletes see this intensively competitive pressure cooker as a context to seek out, not avoid like traditional IO prescription for strategy. After all, under these conditions a young Bhupathi or Sagström face the challenges of stepping up to the professional level. Going hand in hand with the shot at an athletic career is a college education which would hold them in good stead for longer in their life.

Today, Nesty is head coach of the Florida University's Gators swim team. Bhupathi runs tennis centres (MBTA) and is an entrepreneur (Scentials). Sagström is an up and coming professional golfer with some impressive wins to boast.

External Environment in Other Businesses

Frameworks for the analysis of the EE find wide and varied use in carrying out strategic analysis.

Pestel and Uber

The PESTEL framework provides a good starting point for analysing the general EE of a wide variety of businesses, including Uber. Uber attracts political adversaries from taxi unions to drivers with concerns over insurance (P). By dynamically and proximally linking cab drivers to customers who need them, the Uber technology platform reduces costs for customers and increases the earnings potential for cab drivers. Thus, the economic gains created by

Uber are significant (E). A slick app on the ubiquitous smartphone brings the freedom of moving in a city to almost everyone, creating a significant social good (S). The use of real-time geographical information system as well as seamless integration with customer/driver rating system and payment gateway delivers a great technology experience, significant aspects of which are internet protocol protected (T). Proximal and real-time connection of demand supply creates more optimal use to roads and carbon fuels. Ride-sharing aspects of Uber in Indian cities further improves the carbon footprint of the cab ride an individual may take (E). In various jurisdictions across the world—the US, India, China and Europe—the Uber business model threatens and challenges well-entrenched, politically connected interest groups. A woman being raped in an Uber cab in New Delhi brought legal pressures on the company (L).

National Diamond and Top-End Cars

Strategic advantages to luxury brands like Audi, by virtue of their presence in the German luxury car manufacturing industry, can be appreciated by employing the National Diamond model. There is a strong rivalry amongst numerous luxury car manufacturers, driving each to be more innovative and continuously develop high-quality products. Demand conditions in Germany—suburban homeowners, autobahns with no speed limits and a history of innovative, high-power engines—are very conducive for a luxury car brand to flourish. Related and supporting industries play an important role as well. High-quality iron and steel manufacturing, modern banking and finance, component suppliers, IT infrastructure and highly educated work force—all contribute to Audi's competitiveness. Factor conditions conducive for the luxury car manufacturing industry are highly skilled engineers graduating from top-class science and engineering universities and governmental focus on research and development. Across different business contexts, chance or serendipity and government policy also play a key role in a business's success by virtue of being embedded in a competitive National Diamond. This is exactly how the US intercollegiate athletics under the aegis of the NCAA creates a national competitive advantage.

Five Forces and the Entrance Coaching Industry in India

Indians are known to place enormous professional and social importance to the institutions where they earn degrees from. Many entrance-examination-focused coaching centres mushroom in India. How attractive is the industry in which they operate? Porter's Five Forces model can help us answer that question. Suppliers are, typically, highly experienced faculty members, who may also offer entrance coaching of their own. They enjoy a good reputation as well. Signing on better faculty members is a challenge with multiple coaching centres vying for them. Over the last quarter century, a handful of reputed coaching centres, typically regional players, have emerged. Competition amongst them in the local market is intense. When examination results are announced, each of them markets themselves on the basis of the entrance-examination performance of their students. Local rivalry is quite high. Bargaining power of customers is also high, they could choose from various combinations of entrance-coaching offerings. For instance, a student may learn physics from coaching centre A, chemistry and math from B, and biology for C. Threat of new entrants is also high. Local groups of high-quality instructors have the ability to attract students. Threat of substitution is also high. For instance, learning app players like Byju's have introduced adaptive learning technologies that can fine tune the learning experience to each individual student. This is something which is difficult to achieve in the traditional, chalk-and-classroom format. Players like Byju's are venture backed and have a larger war chest to experiment new ideas with. The Five Forces analysis of the entrance-examination coaching industry suggests that the existing players need to be on top of their game to succeed. For Anthony Nesty or Mahesh Bhupathi or Magdalene Sagström, the intensive rivalry of NCAA sport—with new competitors pouring in, only the best getting picked for professional leagues and high-quality college education—this National Diamond creates a great stomping ground for young sportsmen and sportswomen to test their mettle. Benefits for those who make it through this intense scrutiny are not just in terms of successful sports careers but also in terms of valuable capabilities in coaching, talent development and entrepreneurship.

Nascent strategic management was little more than an extension of IO concerns—which businesses to invest in, which industries were profitable in the long run, why and so on. It yielded models and frameworks like PESTEL, National Diamond and Five Forces which help us understand the EE thoroughly. A useful starting point in the study of strategy is innovation, internal organization and EE. In part B, we will examine other equally fascinating strategy lessons. These pertain to blue ocean, leadership, learning, behaviour, networks and the battle of the sexes.

4

Blue Ocean Strategy: Cricket and Celebrities

Marquee sports exist today which weren't around a few decades back. These sports may even be an affront to fans steeped in classical ideas of sports— be it the power, speed and blunt force (trauma) of boxing, or test cricket, or indeed the idea that sports is about outdoor play. Yet MMA, T–20 cricket and e-sports have huge fan following, play in the world's great sporting arenas and dish out big prize monies. How that happens offers valuable 'blue ocean' lessons for strategists. Cirque de Soleil, iTunes and Yellow Tails succeeded explosively employing these strategies in industries as diverse as the circus, information technology and wine—good reasons to learn these blue ocean lessons.

MMA and Universal Fighting Championship (UFC)

Combat sports raise passionate arguments about their inherent brutality. Opponents argue that such wantonly aggressive, blood-thirsty behaviour doesn't have a place in our modern society. Supporters point to the raw aggression, bravery, technique and to the large fan base all across the world. Striking combat sports—boxing, kick-boxing, karate, muay thai, taekwondo—also raise myriad questions about combatant safety. Grappling combat sports—wrestling and judo—are, generally, appreciated for the alacrity and technique on display and are more widely accepted as 'civilized'. But grappling sports have a lower fan following. Many people know of Manny Pacquiao—the boxing champion from Philippines. Only a handful would be able to place their hand on Taha Akgui, the Turk who in 2020 was the reigning Olympic super heavyweight wrestling champion.

Combat sports that combine striking and grappling elements date back to earlier than 1000 BCE in China and to 648 BCE in Ancient Greece, where the sport was called pankration (Gardiner, 1906). In the modern era, interest has endured in a combat spectacle that combined elements of striking and grappling. In 1963, Gene Labell (1963), legendary Judoka, fought the professional boxer Milo Savage in a no-holds-barred fight. Gene Labell had won the US Judo Nationals and Milo Savage was a top-ranked, light heavyweight (pound-for-pound) boxer. Both Labell and Savage were cross-trained and, so, knew what they were going up against, to some extent. Who would you bet on—the judoka or the boxer? The fight happened in Salt Lake City.

> Much against expectations, Labell won the fight in the fourth round after getting Savage in a choke hold. This televised fight was an important point of arrival for MMA.

In the late 1960s and 1970s, the world was introduced to an exhilarating fighting style that incorporated different martial arts styles into one cohesive whole. Even more exhilarating was this style's proponent—the Dragon, Bruce Lee. Bruce Lee had made the transition from martial arts to Hollywood, giving his personal style of MMA great publicity and acceptance. In 1993, 8000 people watched an eight-fighter, single-day tournament in Denver, Colorado—the promotional event of UFC.

> There were no rounds, no judges. Biting and gouging were the only disallowed actions. Fights could end in one of the three ways—submission, knockout or 'towel throw'. While, individually, combat sports had found acceptance, this combination of them was, perhaps, a

little too raw to be accepted in 1993. In various fight jurisdictions, MMA fights were made illegal.

Over time, various 'pure' fighting forms, hybrid forms like Brazilian jiu-jitsu (Andreato et al., 2013) and MMA converged to a system of rules and regulations under the aegis of UFC. Sephamore Entertainment Group (SEG), owned by Bob Meyrowitz (Masucci & Butryn, 2013), was looking to sell off UFC in 2001 when Dana White (Snowden, 2016), an SEG employee, saw the opportunity. He'd convinced his childhood friend, Lorenzo Fertitta, to buy UFC. Lorenzo Fertitta had worked as the commissioner of the Nevada State Athletic Commission, an organization with deep interest in the fight business—most famously, boxing. The Fertitta brothers, Lorenzo and Frank, company Zuffa bought UFC from SEG for $2 million in 2001. They made Dana White the company's president.

UFC built on the pure fighting MMA ethos to make it more mainstream for telecasters, audiences, fighters and regulators. UFC fighters could still use a wide variety of striking and grappling fight techniques.

Normal UFC bouts comprised three five-minute rounds. There are three judges scoring the fight. Fights are now decided by knockout, submission, towel, referee stopping the contest and increasingly, by points.

With the increasing acceptance of MMA and UFC, fighters became more sophisticated and weren't easy to defeat outright via the original mechanisms— submission, knockout, towel—alone. Closer competitions ensued and points awarded by ringside judges became inevitable.

Fights took place in an 'octagon' or 'cage' between fighters belonging to the same weight category. UFC fighters belonged to one of the nine weight categories—straw weight, flyweight, bantamweight, featherweight, lightweight, welterweight, middleweight, light heavyweight and heavyweight. UFC organized, promoted and hosted MMA events or bouts. The advantage of a promotion-based creation of bouts was that bouts that fans loved and cared about could happen more often. The alternative system of a qualification-based scheduling of bouts may be seen to be fairer. In a pay-per-view (PPV) television business model, promotion-based bout schedules held sway. Their disadvantage was the lack of clarity over who 'deserved' to fight whom.

Matchmakers like Joe Silva were complimented for bringing together fighters with contrasting styles, making fights exciting. For example, Anderson Silva versus Fedor Emelianenko (Maher, 2009)—a striker who evolved into a great overall fighter versus a grappler who learned how to strike.

UFC 249 referred to the 249th PPV UFC event. In 2018, there were thirty-nine UFC PPV events hosted, featuring 474 fights. Each event would feature multiple bouts, sometimes, including a championship bout. In 2018, there were about 500 UFC fighters. New, unestablished fighters earned around $10,000 for fight night appearances plus a win bonus. A handful of UFC stars commanded a fight appearance fee of over $500,000. Stars like Conor McGregor have earned $3 million in appearance in a single fight. On 6 October 2018, UFC 229 featuring Khabib versus Conor (Septiana, 2019) reached 2.4 million PPV buys. The average number of PPV buys for UFC events in 2018 was a shade lesser than half a million. UFC events also had a live audience, the highest ever being for UFC 193, featuring Roussey versus Holm on 14 November 2015—56,214!

In 2016, UFC was sold to a group headed by Silver Lake Partners, Kohlberg Kravis Roberts and MSD Capital for over $4 billion. In fifteen years, UFC value had increased by a factor of 2000!

That is not bad for a fighting event which, two decades ago, was gasping for air, fighting for its survival and approval as a mainstream sports event.

T20 Cricket and IPL

IPL, like UFA, is considered to be worth somewhere in the vicinity of $7 billion. T20 cricket started with the marketing manager of the English Cricket Board (ECB), Stuart Robertson, developing the concept of limited overs (twenty overs each) in a cricket match that would last about three hours, just like any big-team sporting contest—soccer, basketball or American football. First introduced by the ECB as a tournament between professional county sides, T20 cricket had an international incubation of over five years. From its 2003 inception, T20 competitions were introduced in Australia, Pakistan and West Indies. Then, almost reluctantly, IPL T20 arrived in India in 2008, after the unofficial Indian Cricket League met an early demise in 2007.

Featuring city-based cricket franchise teams, the IPL became lucrative and featured the best cricketing talent from across the world. So much so that today, IPL has its own window in International Cricket Council's (ICC) Future Tours Program. T20 cricket appealed to a much wider audience than One Day International (ODI) cricket or the archaic test match.

Brought into the fold of cricket fans were more remote followers of the game—many of them women. This greatly increased the commercial value of IPL, in turn increasing the value of players and the excitement on the field, in turn bringing even more fans into the fold, more brands and so on. IPL made the T20 concept a commercial success.

This increased the value of the advertisement slots—be it between overs, during innings changeover, boundary hoardings, on team jerseys and so on.

With telecast infused with entertainment elements like cheerleading and Bollywood celebrities, match audiences reached significantly beyond die-hard cricket fans.

When Lords, the spiritual home of cricket, held its first T20 game, more people came through the turnstiles than any of the more-established formats.

In 2016, the IPL brand (Mitra, 2010) was valued at $4.16 billion and it rocketed to $6.13 billion in 2018. T20 leagues in West Indies, England, Australia and South Africa have all been financial successes. T20 cricket has since proven itself to be not just a profitable icing on the cricket cake, but it has changed the way the game is played, perceived and even who plays it.

Twenty overs have provided cricketers, coaches and commentators an insight into how the risk–reward dynamics change when there are fewer resources (overs) to be considered.

Even the last specialist batsman would take more risks because he/she understood that the tail enders could survive the remaining six overs. Earlier, in a similar situation in a one-day game, the last specialist batsman tended to be more loss averse. Rightly so too, the tail enders could not be trusted to occupy the same percentage of a fifty-overs game—fifteen overs! Given this risk taking, the tail got entrusted with more batting responsibility. 'Nets' featured more opportunities for the tail enders to clear the boundary ropes. In the talent market, the value for a bowler or wicketkeeper, who could strike some meaty blows, increased significantly.

More directly to do with the task of the bowler, there are important upheavals too.

A bowler like J. Bumrah, who hurled the cricket ball at great speeds with variations and skill, may not have gotten the look in if not for his appearance and stellar performance against top-class batsmen in the IPL.

The worry with fast bowlers with unconventional actions, like Bumrah, was that they may suffer frequent injury breakdowns. Mumbai Indians may not have given him a go if not for the fact that he was being tested on his ability to bowl four good, aggressive overs and not ten (ODI) or twenty to thirty over a couple of days (test cricket).

> Just like non-customers were brought into the fold, playing talent that may not have 'made' it—non-resources—were also brought into the fold.

This fresh way of looking at talent applied to veterans just as much as it did to youngsters. On their post ban comeback in 2018, Chennai Super Kings (CSK) reposed faith with veterans—Ambati Rayudu, Harbhajan Singh, Shane Watson, Dwayne Bravo and M.S. Dhoni. Each of them played a stellar role in CSK's victory in that season's IPL—from ashes to glory!

Now, the ICC conducts a T20 Word Cup too—between nations rather than franchise teams. T20 has had a strong influence on the longer formats of the game as well. In one-day competitions, it became quite common for the teams to score upwards of 700 runs in aggregate. To the spectators, this translated into more exciting stroke play, boundary hits and edge of the seat thrills. A similar effect had indeed transpired in test cricket with the advent and establishment of one-day cricket in the 1970s.

Since fourteen Indian players would take to the field in each of the sixty IPL games, it provided a great platform for young Indian cricketers to prove their worth. Young, unheralded Indian cricketers were available at relatively low prices in the player auctions. The market appeared to be giving many up and coming cricketers a chance to prove their worth. When Sachin Tendulkar made his debut for India, it was an acid test—away series against Pakistan back in 1989. Pakistan was then captained, in T20, by their former Prime Minister Imran Khan and featured a young tearaway—Wasim Akram. Akram could move the ball both ways, at great speed and control. Today's Indian cricket talent faces the world's best in the IPL helping them grow confident earlier in their careers as talent development becomes more systematic and broad based.

FBR World Cup

A multiplayer, online video game that was released in 2017 by Epic Games held its first World Cup where players from across the world—40 million of them—strove to notch up points in the individual and team-qualifying competitions. Between April and June 2019, regional qualifiers were held on Saturdays and Sundays, and these events could earn players a ticket to the finals! In FBR, similar to PUBG (Player Unknown's Battlegrounds; Fernandez, 2020), players are parachuted into the battleground zone. When they were dropped, the only equipment they possessed was a pickaxe. Players could collect valuable resources from the ground around them—weapons, food, protection, etc. As the game progressed, the battleground shrank bringing the surviving players/fighters into direct conflict. The last fighter left standing won. Of course, it is not real battle but a peer-to-peer online computer game!

> On the back of being the go-to online video game of a young, technology-savvy generation, FBR had, in 2019, grown into an e-sports rage.

In 2019, the finals of the FBR World Cup were held in Arthur Ashe stadium, the same venue that hosted tennis' US Open finals. Over 24,000 spectators witnessed the finals and Kyle Giersdorf, 'Bugha' (Romo Flores, 2020), won the individual event.

> He took home a cool $7 million prize money much like a US Open winner.

An average FBR match with hundred players would run for around fifteen minutes. Ten minutes if the players were aggressive. Twenty minutes if the player field was packed with conservative players. Points were earned for eliminations (kills of one of the other hundred players) and placement (players remaining on one's elimination). During qualifying, the 40 million runners could play up to ten FBR matches a day. That is about 2.5 hours of intense e-sports action, focused entirely on the gaming console and various FBR parameters to be processed in real time. Continuously forming and updating a three-dimensional mental image out of various two-dimensional stimuli—that's challenging. Right after the drop into the battle zone, kill rates—the frequency with which players are eliminated—could be one every three to four seconds. In comparison, tennis allows twenty seconds between points—there would have been six or seven FBR kills in the time tennis players take to play the next point! As the match progressed, the remaining players, having chalked up valuable resources and being skilled themselves, would be harder to eliminate. Top players may shift focus away from accumulating elimination points to survival and achieving Victory Royale (last player standing, worth ten points).

In the Fortnite World Cup finals at Arthur Ashe stadium (White, 2015) in 2019, players were scored on the points they'd accumulate over six matches. Bugha accumulated fifty-nine points. In each match, should a player achieve the Victory Royale—be the last player standing and eliminate five other players—that player would achieve fifteen points. Over six matches, that is a total of ninety points. Bugha's winning performance in the last FBR World Cup finals clearly indicates intense competition!

Top FBR players are adept at acquiring valuable resources, staying out of trouble (avoid elimination), making kills (eliminating other players), assess risk-reward of various battleground situations and assess skill levels of the remaining players. They need to have great technology and gaming instincts—stamina, alertness, lightning reflexes and sharp decision making.

The 40 million who sought to qualify for the Fortnite World Cup finals, the brands that fronted impressive prize monies and the 24,000 fans who watched the most skilled Fortnite players in the Arthur Ashe stadium should give sceptics a reason to pause.

Epic Games had managed to take the concept made famous by PUBG and scale it into a global e-sports competition. Starting to play FBR is free and has lower hardware requirements as compared to PUBG. This phenomenal growth has been achieved on the back of significant technological innovations in computer and peer-to-peer connectivity. Graphics quality, computing speed, internet bandwidth and gaming consoles were key technical improvements that helped e-sports.

By 2022, e-sports revenues were expected to be $2.7 billion. In 2018, it was almost $900 million. A three-fold increase in just four years and still only a toddler! (Koch, 2019)

The explosive growth of these sporting extravaganzas (UFC, IPL and Fortnite) is on the back of wins in three key areas. First is the continuous exploration and refinement of opportunities in the gaps between established boundaries (UFC). Second is the redesign to reach out to non-customers as well as non-resources and the pursuit to improve customer value significantly (IPL). Third is the simultaneous pursuit of both cost reductions and differentiation (Fortnite) leading to rapid market growth and customer engagement. These ideas were developed by Kim Chan and Renee Marborgne in their theory of Blue Ocean Strategy (BOS). BOS provides us with various tools and frameworks that can be employed to identify business blue oceans.

Blue Ocean Strategy

Kim Chan and Renee Mauborgne introduced BOS (Mauborgne & Kim, 2005) in 2005. BOS offers unique points of departure from traditional economic and strategic thinking (which focused on how to win in red oceans). BOS offers tools and frameworks that could be employed by organizations to create their respective BOS.

BOS is distinct from red ocean thinking in that it focuses on creating uncontested market space (not competing in existing market space), making the competition irrelevant (not beating the competition), creating and capturing new demand (not exploiting existing demand), breaking the value–cost trade-off (not making the value–cost trade-off) and aligning the whole system to deliver differentiation and low cost (not delivering differentiation *or* low cost). For managers, searching out the most promising ideas is difficult to do, and BOS offers ways in which managers can search for these game-changing ideas. The Six Paths framework (Lindgren et al., 2010) helps them examine blue ocean possibilities in a thorough fashion. The Six Paths to identifying high-potential blue oceans are looking across industry boundaries, looking across strategic groups within an industry, redefining the industry buyer group, looking across complementary product and service offerings, rethinking the functional-emotional orientation of the industry and consciously participating in shaping (rather than just responding to) industry trends. The ERRC grid (Gündüz, 2018; eliminate, reduce, raise and create) can be used by decision makers to rigorously examine opportunities to create blue oceans. Value innovation (Kim & Mauborgne, 2005) captures the synchronized increase of buyer utility and decrease of cost. Value innovation calls for the redesign of the organization's strategy canvas. Strategy canvas is nothing but the plot of offerings' relative levels of features against the reference offering, typically the blue ocean concept.

BOS in Action

Here, we discuss the frameworks introduced, namely, Six Paths framework, ERRC and value innovation in the three sporting contexts of UFC, IPL and FBR, respectively.

Six Paths Framework and UFC

MMA in its UFC avatar asked fundamental questions about the nature of combat sports. It drew inspiration from existing combats like Brazilian jiu-jitsu and held on the fundamental aspects of honest fighting and remained method agnostic. Honest fighting eschews means like gouging and biting or violence like kicking a floored opponent. By employing this loose hand, UFC allowed MMA to define itself through discovery of pockets between the more established striking and grappling fighting techniques. UFC, thereby, unshackled the sheer diversity of fighting techniques. PPV television dynamics ensure tightly coupled feedback for the UFC events being put together. Traditional fights tend to have stars emerge in specific weight categories and, once in a while, great rivalries developed. Fights featuring the stars or rivalries or championship bouts are heavily followed. Boxing fights like Oscar De La Hoya versus Manny Pacquiao were followed all over the world! However, majority of fights did not get the same fan following. In UFC, the distinct and, sometimes, contrasting fighting styles introduced another key fight dimension that promoters, organizers and broadcasters worked with—striking- and grappling-based fighters.

ERRC Framework and IPL

IPL refined Stuart Robertson's original idea by eliminating elements that placed the highest challenge to cricket's acceptance as a mass-market, big team extravaganza. Making for a short, compact evening sport drove the elimination of 'unnecessary' middle overs that ate up a lot of the time in the ODIs. IPL brought highly skilful players to the T20 format and what this meant was that the promise of exciting cricket set up by the format was fulfilled. The short format set the stage, but bringing the high-quality talent was crucial in unlocking the potential for big-hitting, skilful bowling and athleticism on the cricket field. Thereby IPL raised the sheer excitement inherent in a game of cricket. By bringing celebrities and fanfare to cricket, IPL introduced elements that made cricket no longer a sport only for the stoic. It proved to be successful in reaching out to erstwhile non-cricket fans. It also proved to be successful in giving a chance to erstwhile non-resources—youngsters at the periphery and veterans. Simultaneously, more consumers and consumer brands flocked the game as cricket left its traditional, largely male audiences to attract the attention of women as well as anybody who found IPL cricket exciting, which many did.

Value Innovation and Fortnite

An exemplar for value innovation—simultaneous leaps in cost and differentiation—can be seen in Epic

Games' FBR. With the continued fall in computing hardware costs, even specialist gaming machines are available at about the cost of a 200 cc motorbike in India. For millennials and Gen Zs, a gaming console investment became plausible. Going from playing with friends, Fortnite brought exciting international competition, matching wits, tactics, strategy, reflexes— all quintessential to athletic struggles. Fortnite World Cup's qualifications in 2019 stand testimony to the fact that this was a competition, not just a video game for leisure. About 40 million players took a stab, over two months, at qualifying for the finals of the 2019 FBR World Cup. No wonder then that brands flocked to be visible to the fastest growing demographic— Gen Z—one about which much is argued and little understood. No wonder the FBR finals happened in tennis' hallowed Arthur Ashe stadium, witnessed by 24,000 spectators. No wonder then that the Fortnite singles champion of 2019, sixteen-year-old Bugha, took home prize money of $7 million, right up there with any professional sport.

BOS in Other Businesses

BOS thinking finds resonance with a wide range of business contexts. Here, we discuss the same three frameworks of BOS—Six Paths, ERRC and value innovation—in the context of the circus, technology and wine industries, respectively.

Cirque de Soleil and Six Paths Framework

Cirque de Soleil managed to reinvent the circus by systematically questioning existing definitions of the circus industry.

Were animals jumping though fire rimmed hoops essential for the circus? No. Cirque de Soleil looked across the circus to concerts and music shows for big-draw, theatrical ideas. Would patrons pay for more sophisticated, orchestrated music, acrobatics and lights? Yes. The emotional appeal of the circus had the animals and circus artists at its base. Would patrons—more the parents than the kids—respond positively to the emotional appeal being generated through scored music and orchestra? Yes. Rather than reacting to animal rights activists' demonstrations, Cirque proactively reduced the role of animals. It drove the circus industry trend rather than being simply subject to it. By asking these fundamental questions, as suggested by the Six Paths framework, Cirque de Soleil managed to reinvent the circus profitably in the 1980s. The circus was no longer simplistic entertainment mainly for children but targeted to gain approval of the parents' more sophisticated palate, which kids enjoyed just as thoroughly.

iTunes and ERRC Grid

iTunes eliminated the record label, a very powerful entity that dictated, along with radio and TV stations, which music and musicians were able to reach the listener. iTunes unbundled music. It wasn't necessary to purchase an entire album if the listener was only interested in a couple of tracks. iTunes also significantly increased personal, earphone-listening to music. This was achieved through great design and performance of music accessories. Along with the ubiquitous cell phone and in continuation of the Walkman revolution, music was now consumed in commute and work settings just as much as in leisurely and private settings.

In 2004, U2 used the first single of their *How to Dismantle an Atomic Bomb* album, 'Vertigo', to promote iPod and iTunes. Apple's iTunes not only dealt with the problem of music piracy but also allowed music listeners and artists to determine prices of singles on the high-quality iTunes platform. This made the music listener directly accessible to the artist, rather than through a music label, with its own artistic and commercial predilection.

Yellow Tail and Value Innovation

When the Castella family launched its Yellow Tail 750 ml wine bottles in the US (2001), it performed a lot better than expected. Yellow Tail was priced a little higher than the budget wines. Its branding eschewed fancy wine terminology, broad marketing, focus on wine aging, complexity and vineyard prestige. It had been these factors that hitherto separated budget and premium wines. Yellow Tail targeted a wider range of palates especially for those new to wine, bottle selection was made easy with very few options (red and sparkling) and built fun and adventurous brands. Yellow Tail achieved value innovation given the significant cost reductions as well as market and pricing growth of the above strategies.

In the first year of their US launch, 200,000 cases were sold against the expected 25,000 cases. By the end of 2005, Yellow Tail had sold a cumulative of 25 million cases in just five years!

Blue ocean thinking is indeed an important part of the strategist's repertoire!

5

Strategic Learning: Good to Great!

At the highest sporting echelons, it is quite often that an 'unstoppable force' meets an 'immovable object'. Being able to win these high-voltage competitions and lay claim to greatness requires sportsmen and sportswomen to learn, unlearn and relearn. It isn't as easy as it may seem. It is human to cling to past victories and habits—after all, they got you here! Be it a chess grandmaster (GM), a master soccer tactician or boxing's Magnificent Mary, this journey to greatness is hard and the learning difficult. Just ask the top-management consultants in the world!

GM to Five-Time World Chess Champion

In 1988, Vishwanathan Anand became chess GM at the age of eighteen years. Even before he became GM, embryonic computational and technology support were available in barter for his encyclopaedic knowledge of chess games. Frederic Friedel, a German chess fan and pioneer of ChessBase would throw open his first-cut chess program for Anand to explore. It was run on an Atari ST 8 MHz Motorola CPU, back in 1987! Anand would make impressive progress as a GM and in only six years as GM, by 1995, he was challenging Garry Kasparov for the title of World Chess Champion. The match was played in the 107th-floor observation deck of the World Trade Center, New York. It was a classic chess match of twenty games, over five weeks, four games a week, with the first player to 10.5 points winning. Two weeks of the match done, something remarkable was unfolding. The young Indian challenger kept up; the score was 4–4 after eight draws. Anand scored a memorable win in the ninth game to start off the third week with a bang.

But he then fell apart to lose the match 10.5–7.5. Kasparov, at the age of thirty-four, became sixth-time world champion. In 1998, Anand took on Kasparov's rival through the 1980s–90s—Anatoly Karpov. But he came up short yet again.

By this time, with two failed attempts at the summit under his belt, there were murmurs if Anand would be the best chess player never to be world champion.

Whether he was too nice, whether he lacked the killer instinct to win big and so on. In his 2019 book *Mind Master*, he goes on to reveal that,

'The transition from being a strong player to becoming a champion wasn't going to happen on its own.' (Anand, 2019, pp. 116–17)

He had probably become 'too predictable a player', having committed the rookie mistake of 'not switching openings' and thereby becoming a sitting duck. Unlike top chess tournaments where each GM focused on how to do well against the whole field, in World Championships, players have one opponent to focus upon. This involves more than high-quality chess. There is a complex chess meta-game to contend with. What openings would surprise my opponent? How might my opponent plan to surprise me? And so on.

GMs competing for the championship have a team of 'seconds'—accomplished chess players—working tirelessly in the background so the championship contender is better prepared to take on the opponent. Mandates given to the team of seconds, and individual seconds are of crucial importance. One may be tasked with researching an opponent's favourite opening lines and themes. Another may be tasked with coming up with attacking ideas around which the GM could surprise the opponent. Yet another could be tasked with 'breaking down' meticulously developed openings. This breaking down and/or failure to do so would greatly enhance the GM's confidence to deal with important in-game situations.

Be it the arrival of strong chess programs or artificial intelligence (AI) in chess (Brooks, 1990) and concomitant cheaper, high-quality computer hardware, being good with technology fast became a key competitive edge in chess. Early chess development advantaged those who knew the Russian language because chess theory was developed in Russian books. Similarly, technology comfort has provided a significant edge to the current stars like Caruana and Carlsen. Computers may well think many steps ahead on a particular path, but as Anand explains, it is, perhaps, more important to think broad and an adequate number of steps ahead. These number of steps may not necessarily be a large number simply because of the many imponderables—opponent making a great move, opponent making a mistake, etc.—that can intervene to make narrow, thinking-ahead not that fruitful.

'Once you've assessed the resources at your disposal and weighed what is feasible against what is risky you will see the path' (Brooks, 1990, p. 163). The chess legend Jose Raul Capablanca was asked how many moves ahead he thought. His answer was simple. 'Only one, but it's the right one!'

Anand would break the jinx and win the first of his five World Chess Championships in 2000. When Anand led Kramnik in the 2008 World Chess Championship in Bonn, he improved a great deal when it came to handle a lead and the meta-game. Rather than lapse into passive, automatic play, he was able to build a big lead of three points and go on to win the championship. This was achieved by being unafraid to anticipate opponent moves and spring a surprise or two of his own.

Anand's professional career, stretching from the 1980s till 2020, stands testimony to him dealing well with big changes—globalization and internationalization of chess as well as the influential role computer technology and AI would play in chess—all after starting out with books. Right from the first (failed) assault in 1995, Ubilava would be a prominent organizational member of Anand's team of seconds. Patrick Wolff, Jon Speelman, Artur Yusupov and Peter Leko were Anand's seconds in the 1990s. From 2000 onwards, Radoslaw Wojtaszek (Radek)— also Anand's protégé, Grzegorz Gajewski, Surya Sekhar Ganguly and Sandipan Chanda—all high-quality, young GMs—would bring their creativity and hard work to the task of Anand winning World Championships. From 2002 to 2012, the Danish GM, Peter Heine Nielsen, coached Anand to four World Championship wins.

In 2010, rumours flew around during the Sofia World Championship match that Veselin Topalov had many super computers at his disposal. Top GMs like Kramnik and Carlsen would volunteer to help Anand train. Anand would also get access to multiple, distributed chess servers where the chess engine simulations could be run. Anand would eventually get the better of Topalov in the 2010 World Chess Championship match.

Assistance for the 2000 World Championship match in Tehran against Alexi Shirov would arrive not only from great chess minds and technology. Pablo San Segundo Carrillo (Pablo) would join Anand's camp, his contribution being the lightening up of the training sessions!

Josep 'PEP' Guardiola: Spain to Germany to England

When Guardiola (Violan, 2014) took over the coaching mantle in 2008–09 at the first team of FCB, total football had come a full generational cycle. Pep had been, as a player, handpicked by Cruyff (Sports Bureau, 2017) and come to embody total football principles—spatial awareness and intelligence, interchanges and ball control.

La Liga to Bundesliga to English Premier League (EPL)

Just like many players of the golden FCB generation (Prithingar, 2018)—Xavi, Iniesta, Messi, Busquets, Piqué, Pedro and Puyol—Pep was very young, just thirteen when he came to La Masia, FCB's 'farm' for developing promising, young players. As a player for Barcelona and Spain, Guardiola developed into an astute central, mid-field player 'pulling the strings'. He featured in league winning teams for FCB (six times), European Cup winning team (once) and won the gold medal in the Barcelona Olympics of 1992. He captained for a number of seasons.

He would return to coach the FCB B team in 2007–08, taking over senior team coaching from Frank Rijkaard (Soriano, 2012) the subsequent season. In the four seasons from 2008–09 to 2011–12, Pep would lead the golden FCB generation to remarkable, on-field successes, firmly institute his own stamp on modern, total football, identify remarkable player talent and set the ground for his own influential and successful coaching career.

He let go of the superstars on the FCB payroll (Ronaldinho, Ibrahimović) to make way for the sorts of players he envisioned could succeed playing his brand of total football, amongst them were Dani Alves, Seydou Keita and Gerard Piqué.

Dipping into the talent development ecosystem, Cantera, Busquets and Pedro were promoted to the first team. Under the on-field leadership of an earlier class of La Masia—Messi, Xavi, Iniesta, Puyol—Pep would unleash the Tiki Taka (Luo et al., 2013). It was a system of ball retention, high defensive lines and featuring ball playing defenders and even goalkeepers like Victor Valdez. These were, obviously, huge risks too. FCB prided itself on its philosophy, but poor performances were never looked upon kindly. With a group of players who had inculcated the skills and philosophies from a very young age, Pep would helm a successful Barcelona generation. In four seasons, they won three league titles and two Champions League titles.

German Bundesliga

After four seasons in FCB and a year-long US sabbatical, he'd coach Bayern Munich (Gillmeister, 2000) in the German Bundesliga (Bühler, 2006). Being a storied club with its own, more direct, successful methods, the ball possession philosophy wasn't understood just as readily in Bayern. An example is the early experiences with the 'rondo', a drill where players stood on the circumference of an imaginary circle, passing the ball with a single touch and two or three players inside the circle who strove to win the ball/disrupt the rondo. In the initial days, Phillip Lahm and Manuel Neuer were in the minority of players who took the rondo seriously. After all, it was a drill used mainly to warm up for practice sessions.

> The rondos (Clarke, 2019) quickly revealed to Bayern players that consistent ball possession was the outcome of astute positional play. If all the players of the team didn't position themselves in relation to the ball carrier, opponents and spaces, then ball retention would be quite difficult.

Faced with injuries to key players, Pep infused new players who could lead Bayern down Pep's philosophical path. For example, Joshua Kimmich came into the squad as centre half and not as central midfielder. Kimmich's shift was accompanied by Lahm (a defender) pushing up to the centre circle, joining Xabi Alonso in the middle of the park. This left Kimmich— his central defence partner, Badstuber and the other full back, Bernat to bring the ball up the field—soon to be joined by Lahm and Alonso. While Bayern played with four defenders, they shifted patterns when they had the ball, enabling more precise passes because the five players were much closer to each other than four could be.

Pep's teams played 4–4–2 or 4–3–3 when they did not have the ball. When they did have the ball, they played 3–5–2, creating many attacking opportunities and making it difficult for opponents to close down passing channels.

> Over the three seasons he had at Bayern, players became comfortable with the new system. Bayern already had a great squad with player potential under the previous coach, Heyneckes.

At the base of the Pep philosophy was a goalkeeper good enough to play in the team as an outfield player (Murphy, 2020). Goalkeepers, who were comfortable and competent with their feet, allowed the team to stretch its forces over a larger part of the field. This created more spaces for making runs and passes. This also placed enormous stress on the opponent's energies. Chasing down passes played between the opponent's defenders sapped the energies of the attacking players. When Germany won the World Cup in Brazil, its goalkeeper, Manuel Neuer completed more passes than Lionel Messi!

EPL

Pep moved to coaching Manchester City of the EPL in the 2015–16 season. City under Pep would smash league points records, finishing the 2017–18 season with 100 points! Especially in the physical style of the EPL and its intense competitiveness, City's 2017–18 season performance was stand-out. Winning 84 per cent of games in a competitive, crowded league was quite a task. Pep inherited a squad whose transfer market price was over $1 billion! Earning buy-ins from all the stakeholders to play a collective game in such a super, star environment wasn't easy.

Guardiola continued to, relentlessly, apply possession football principle in City. At the same time, when ball possession was lost, there were more players in positions to win back possession quickly, reset and return to dominating the opponent. What some referred to in Barcelona as the six-second rule still applied. Win back possession quickly or reset into the defensive formation.

> The offside rule played a crucial role as well. A player cannot be offside while receiving a ball kicked by his/her goalkeeper from the penalty box. What this meant was that opponents would have to leave defenders in their own half to contend with goalkeepers capable of delivering long, accurate aerial passes.

When Ederson Santana De Moraes (Ducker, 2017), the twenty-three-year-old Brazilian, was bought by City in 2017–18 from Benfica, that was exactly the capability added to the City arsenal. Ederson was tasked with roaming his entire half when his team was on attack. Having played as an outfield player early in his career, Ederson genuinely believed he (the goalie) was the start of attack. His long passes reaching into the opponent's half ensured the opponent couldn't commit more players to attack. This was reminiscent of the Dani Alves, then FCB right-back, pointing out that a big part of his defensive duties lay in the amount of attacking he did. Much like Victor Valdez or Claudio Bravo or Manuel Neuer, Ederson developing in Pep's tutelage defined the modern goalkeeper in soccer.

The ideas being developed and implemented by pioneering managers and coaches like Pep Guardiola would become business as usual and widely implemented in a few years. Until rivals catch up, teams like FCB would haul in rich rewards. The players on the field, when these ideas were being implemented, made a huge leap—away from what has always worked for them, towards uncertainty and excitement. Top managers were able to enthuse their players by appealing to their athletic side, showing significant improvements and allowing them to experience winning.

> A twenty-four-year-old Ederson invests in a long, successful career of, say, fifteen years. What better way of doing so than to be at the head of the change that would become industry standard!

Magnificent Mary

Mary Kom's story has humble beginnings in Manipur. Her parents were tenant farmers and quite poor. She was born in 1983. When she was fifteen, Dingko Singh of the same state would win a gold medal in boxing in the Asian Games. This spurred on the teenage girl who boxed without her parents even knowing about it. Once she started winning local competitions, the secret that she was a talented boxer could not be kept further. At the age of fifteen, she began to train under coach K. Kosana Meitei in Imphal. It is here that her strong boxing basics and stronger will came to be noticed.

At the age of eighteen, in 2001, she won a silver medal in the Amateur International Boxing Association World Boxing Championships in the US in the 48 kg category. By 2010, Kom had amassed five World Boxing Championship gold medals. In the intervening years, she'd married and given birth to twins in 2007. In 2012 London Olympics, she stepped up the weight categories and boxed in the under 51 kg, flyweight category. She won bronze, having lost in the semis to the eventual gold medallist. Mary Kom is the only woman who has won six World Boxing Championship golds. Through her career, she fought great odds to come through the boxing ranks, to stay there post child-birth (at twenty-four and thirty-one), and keep winning. Kom also stepped up the weight categories from 46, 48 kg light flyweight division to the 51 kg flyweight division. This has allowed her to compete in the Olympics. Moving up and down weight categories has a direct impact on the relative speed, power, flexibility and energy of the boxer. Her consistent wins over a decade and a half have earned her the title of Magnificent Mary. Through the many episodes of naysaying, Kom has been steadfast in her trust when it comes to being a champion boxer.

The challenges she has faced have been to do with coming from a poor state of a developing country, a state faced with militant insurgency, societal misogyny when it comes to a woman athlete and bouncing back from two childbirths to the top of a punishing, professional sport.

The only things that she has to say to the doubters are medals. With eight, she has one more World Boxing Championship medal than the Cuban great, Felix

Illustration 5.1: Magnificent Mary

Savon! She has been the one constant in her weight category—light flyweight (48 kg), bravely stepping up to the flyweight during the Olympics. Mary Kom, Magnificent Mary, continued to fly the flag into Tokyo.

Double-Loop Learning

Between 1974 and 1978, David Schon and Chris Argyris (1996) developed their 'theories of action' and 'double-loop learning' (Argyris, 1977). Action proceeds in three steps: (a) understanding of the governing variables of action, (b) action strategies for the actor and (c) consequences on actor. Two important consequences of such action are (a) on learning and (b) effectiveness.

Single-loop learning (Korth, 2000) involves the analysis and redesign of the second action step—action strategies for the actor. An example is how a thermostat works. On measuring that the current temperature is higher (lower) than the target room temperature, the air conditioning system switches on (off). Single-loop learning is quite operational and good competitors all do reasonably well at this. Double-loop learning is more challenging in that an error between expected and actual outcome triggers an evaluation of the first action step, understanding the governing variables of action. In our thermostat example, it may trigger a re-evaluation of whether the ambient temperature is so high (low) that the thermostat's target temperature ought to be different. Double-loop learning is strategic and even good competitors may go astray when it comes to assessing the governing variables themselves.

Model I thinking is characterized by the following governing variables of action: (a) achieving of purposes as I see them, (b) maximize winning, minimize losing and minimize eliciting of negative emotions, and (c) rationality and minimization of emotions. Model II thinking, on the other hand, is characterized by (a) valid information basis, (b) free and informed choice and (c) internal commitment to choice and ongoing monitoring of implementation. Model I thinking has single-loop learning as its learning outcome whereas Model II thinking can lead to double-loop learning.

Double-Loop Learning in Action

Here, we discuss three important characteristics of double-loop learning—valid information, minimally defensive interpersonal and group dynamics, and frequent testing of theories publicly. These double-loop learning characteristics are seen in Vishwanathan Anand's journey to five-time World Chess Champion, Pep Guardiola's career as a professional soccer manager and six-time World Boxing Champion Mary Kom, respectively.

Valid Information and Vishwanathan Anand

The teams supporting the GMs in the World Chess Championship match have a direct relationship to outcomes in the individual games. The coach and the seconds play a huge role in preparing the GM in terms of novelties to attempt as well to expect. At the highest level, chess is highly intricate and complex, going many levels deeper than what it appears on the surface. The only way to perceive these levels and prepare is through high-powered teams, each with a specific domain of supremely high expertise. For instance, specific openings and gambits, design of lines of play, historical game knowledge, simulation of AI versus AI, a spirit that can lighten the mood and so on.

GM seconds also need to gel very well together in order to survive the pressures and outperform. Amidst all this complexity, risks need to be taken in order to win. Anand reveals how this risk taking is finally the GM's call. That said, if a gambit designed/suggested by a second works badly, it is very important for the GM to not just face the consequences but also to support that particular second. His or her whose next idea may well be the winner.

In the rarefied and high-expertise environment of chess, it is that much more of a challenge to assemble and maintain a team that works well together. Anand's long reign at the top of chess suggests that he has been able to keep valid information and good ideas flowing. He has been able to maintain a team that sees value in getting back together for another assault. This is a remarkable managerial or leadership achievement.

Without a coherent seconds environment, a GM at the board may not come across anywhere as brilliant!

Group Dynamics and PEP Guardiola

Guardiola (Kleinert et al., 2012) helped develop a learning-oriented team dynamic in the diverse professional clubs that he has coached. Having been a top international player himself, a number of the novel interventions started on the training pitch. These are tightly related to the sort of football he expects his teams to play and succeed at. Be it the attention paid to the 'rondo' or a goalkeeper who doubles as a sweeper back, Guardiola succeeded in instilling in top players a better, novel way to go about winning football matches. This not only helped the club win but also made them better players, with higher market valuations. Further, the philosophy helped their national teams do better and build on player strengths. Building on player strengths started much before the pitch—in the trading rooms, where specific types of player talent is sought. Be it Kimmich in Bayern or Ederson in Manchester City, this joint development approach of Guardiola has worked consistently well. The governing variable here is the free and informed choice made by everyone—club owners to player talent—to go about competing on the field in a certain (total football) way.

Frequent Tests and Mary Kom

Between 2001 and 2010, Mary Kom established herself in the light flyweight division, winning six golds and one silver in the World Boxing Championships. Since 2010, she has been gradually testing herself in the flyweight division. The Olympic bronze in London (2012) and a disappointing DNQ in Rio (2016) have seen her commit to the 51 kg class. The thirty-seven-year-old veteran qualified for Tokyo-frequent tests through the years appear to have prepared her for this big challenge—the Olympic flyweight competition.

In 2019, she won bronze at the World Boxing Championships in the flyweight division, boosting her confidence for the Olympics. 'I think I did very well overall. It is perfect now, yeah it is precious' (PTI, 2019b). Mary Kom appeared confident to take on the field in Tokyo in 2020 (2021). After her performance in the 51 kg of the 2019 World Boxing Championships, she reflected:

> It has made things easier for me in terms of planning for Olympics. I had never fought the girls I fought this time and you know what, I think it wasn't all that difficult beating them. So I have got a good idea of what awaits me in the Olympics . . . and I now have the confidence that I can beat that.

The frequent and public testing of Mary Kom's decisions are in the ring. Her performances help her gauge how she is keeping up with the younger, taller fighters. Her stepping up to the flyweight category in the Olympics and Asian stages have helped her learn critical aspects of fighting against bigger, stronger boxers. These experiences also strengthen her resolve and commitment towards winning Olympic gold (governing variable). Rather than being defensive of her stature as a six-time World Boxing Championship gold medallist, she is in a learning and growth-oriented exploration of higher challenges—51 kg flyweight and the Olympics!

Double-Loop Learning in Other Businesses

Double-loop learning episodes can be seen in a number of business contexts. They are 37signals led by Jason Fried and David Chang's refocusing of his successful restaurant chain. These are examples of key double-loop learning ingredients. These ingredients are the governing variable of valid information, the actor driving through minimally defensive interpersonal and group dynamics, and the learning consequence of publicly testing hypothesis, respectively.

Valid Information: 37signals

Most organizations stick to the five-day week, a schedule designed for Industrial Revolution factory work, and whose efficacy, in the modern information age, has hardly been tested. This may not cause any obvious problems but is not necessarily the smartest way to do things either. We may be ignoring an important lever to improve organizational creativity significantly.

37signals, under the leadership of its CEO, Jason Fried, started experimenting with how a work week might look like. A variety of ideas were tried out—four-day weeks, thirty-two-hour weeks, an entire summer month off—all with a view to explore new ideas. Business, as usual, practices like long meetings were cut back on. Quiet workspaces were created. Over time, what worked and what didn't would become obvious. Many organizations—3M, Google included—engage in these experiments and set policy on the basis of valid information rather than dogma. The essence of these changes is the organizational willingness to base policy off of valid information. This is akin to Anand's team and his preparation that led to five World Chess Championship wins.

Group Dynamics: Chang's

Chang knew his cooking was excellent, but how could he make his restaurant profitable? His early setbacks were the type from which many people wouldn't recover, they may simply give up. But Change was different, he started a process of making honest self-assessments. This self-assessment included the business' foundational belief that the restaurant should serve only noodles. Surprisingly, Chang decided to make a significant change to the menu, introducing a good number of items that were not noodles. Taking this risk paid off; 'the crowds came, rave reviews piled up, awards followed and unimaginable opportunities presented themselves'. This is what double-loop learning looks like in action: questioning everything and starting from scratch, if necessary. This is akin to Josep Guardiola building a certain 'total football' philosophy in the teams he coaches. The trust in the system/solution opens up the canvas and the floor to discussions, personnel and trainings that unlock value and even change industry.

Frequent and Public Testing of Hypothesis: Argyris and Schon Workshops

Argyris and Schon conducted workshops for managers from a number of organizations with the objective to understand and release the main blocks to double-loop learning. One exercise was for the departmental heads in a multi-department manufacturing organization facing strife between finance managers and line heads. Each of the heads was asked to write down how they would communicate to the others about a high inventory problem faced in the organization. On the right column of the page would be the actual, official communication that would be made. On the left column of the page would be the 'mind-voice'—what departmental heads were actually thinking about. After collecting this from all the heads—line managers and finance professionals—comparisons of the right and left columns were made and discussed. This showed just how few of the individual hypotheses were tested publicly. In fact, a lot of the noting on the left column assumed that the others (line managers/finance professional) would not get my (finance professionals/ line managers) viewpoint at all. It would require great energy to escape from this thinking trap. This is akin to Mary Kom consistently going up against the best in the world, not just in her 'native' light flyweight but also in the Olympic flyweight division, continually testing her mettle towards where she was headed.

Careful reflection of individual learning orientation and organizational learning dynamics is crucial for strategists and managers to be able to guide their organization in choppy waters. Just as the turbulence and challenges facing the business and the world, at large, increase, those who—individuals and organizations—learn better stand a better chance to succeed.

6

The Lustrous Strategic Leadership

The Italian soccer manager, Ranieri, gave a young Moroccan attacker Mahrez an expanded responsibility to win games for Leicester City in the 2015–16 EPL. It was just one instance of heroes emerging for Leicester during that season. Eventually, the 5000:1 underdog won the league! Inspiring such remarkable performances are managers, coaches and leaders. The effect they have on their team is there for all to see. Be it Gregg Popovich or Billie Jean King or Claudio Ranieri, they share a deep concern for performance and for their people, irrespective of their individual leadership styles. This is seen in the remarkable business leadership of Hastings (Netflix), Buffett (Berkshire Hathaway) and Schulz (Starbucks).

Gregg Popovich at the San Antonio Spurs

The 1992 Barcelona Olympics was the first time NBA players represented the US. Interest in international basketball grew and the spotlight also fell on top players outside the US. In 1990, the starting day rosters of the thirty NBA teams had less than 5 per cent international players. Popovich had been assistant coach of the San Antonio Spurs for just one season under Larry Brown when he travelled overseas to watch the 1989 European Basketball Championships. On court in the finals for the then Yugoslavia were six players who would go on to NBA careers! Even then there were few other NBA personnel scouting for talent.

It was quite common for young basketball players in Europe to come through six hours of coaching a day during camps. The grind instilled a strong team ethic in them. In comparison, an entitled mindset dominated American basketball talent and it led to underdevelopment of their team-basketball skills.

Popovich was among the first in the NBA to understand this phenomenon of an international basketball player. He put an entire team basketball philosophy, with a significant international playing roster, into action at an NBA franchise—the San Antonio Spurs.

The 2012–13 NBA opening night roster of the Spurs included eight players (more than 50 per cent) from outside of the US. In 1996, the Spurs faced injury troubles and poor performance. They finished the regular season with an abysmal record. Finishing at the bottom of the league meant that they got a higher chance in the next season's first round lottery for top college players. They won the lottery and picked a twenty-year-old Tim Duncan from the US Virgin Islands. He would, under Popovich, go on to win five NBA titles in a nineteen-year career.

After a run to the 1972 Olympic trials and intelligence stints in the US Army, Popovich had returned to basketball coaching at a small, Division III college team. Despite a disastrous first season, he went about building a strong squad by careful analysis of the high-school player market. In 1986, he became assistant coach of Larry Brown at the Spurs.

> Extensively talking to high school coaches, he built up a list of good players who could help his team win but not so talented that they would aspire to go somewhere better.

From the mid-1990s onwards, Popovich built a world-class basketball team; Manu Ginobli from Argentina and Tony Parker from France would join Tim Duncan from the US Virgin Islands.

This hard work was the foundation on which he commanded respect from his players. He'd watch films of games just as thoroughly as he expected players to be switched on at practice. Popovich encouraged, demanded that players read widely and form a rich world view.

He'd give books for players to read—something quite unusual for a professional basketball coach to do. It was a stark contrast to the thinking that great players were built through relentless practice and single-mindedness.

Popovich worked on a different principle. Great players were built through empathy and a rich worldview. He not only challenged his team as basketball players but also as learners.

Players who achieved great success under Popovich, like Steve Kerr and Tim Duncan, would return to coaching. Popovich didn't shy away from giving credit of the Spurs' successes to other coaches. In amongst these great qualities of Popovich as a leader is the standout performance he drove. He maintained a win rate of 85 per cent—very hard to achieve in a league like the NBA which institutes many mechanisms to keep the playing field level.

> He led the Spurs for over two decades, leading them to five NBA championships!

Popovich's leadership was transformational. He had changed the places from where top-player talent was sourced. Rather than individual style and showmanship, what was emphasized was the team. Even the all-star who played under Popovich, Tim Duncan, was celebrated for his team contributions. He averaged only 19 points a game—not necessarily legend material in most other teams, under most other coaches.

Billie Jean King

Women face tougher challenges than the men in many walks of life. Before we start discussing Billie Jean King's leadership of the Original 9 (Schultz, 2011) and what they did half a century back, it is important to get a sense of where professional women's sport was in 2020. Nate Silver, the NBA commissioner, said that WNBA (Women's National Basketball Association) was not marketed well enough. Elena Delle Donne, a star WNBA player, agreed with Nate Silver in identifying it as a marketing issue, but pointed out that it's not so much the quality of marketing as it is the marketing budget. WNBA just didn't gain access to the mountain of resources that the NBA did.

David Berri, professor of economics in Southern Utah University, pointed out two fundamental differences between men's sport and women's sport. First was media coverage and second was political support. Fans were much more likely to follow the sport/league that dominated the sports media and they were much more likely to flock modern, well-designed and easy-to-access stadia. Key to the former was marketing budget and key to the latter was political support.

In the US, 75 per cent of sports media coverage was dedicated to men's basketball, football and baseball. Only 5 per cent of sports media coverage was dedicated to women's sports (Wilson, 1991). A 2016 study of Indian newspapers showed that less than 5 per cent of the sports coverage was for women's sports. In 2014, WNBA and MLS (Major League Soccer) had average, per-game TV viewership of 240,000 and 222,000, respectively. Nevertheless, MLS's TV deal paid $75 million, three times more than the NBA TV deal. Basically, MLS got more free publicity than WNBA. This is notwithstanding the fact that WNBA is a premier women's basketball league whereas MLS is diminutive compared to the top soccer leagues of Europe and South America. When it came to political support, $800 million of taxpayer subsidies were provided to the MLS and $15 billion to the big men's professional sports (Paulsen, 2020)—much,

much larger than the support provided to all the big American women's sports leagues put together.

So, that is the snapshot of the uneven playing field faced by professional women's sports, in 2019, in the US. So, can we imagine how it must have been back in 1970, half a century ago?

Back then, the Open era in tennis had allowed professionals and brought money into the sport. But things weren't much better for the women. The 1970 men's US Open champion got paid $20,000 whereas the women's champion won $7,500. It would be another two years till Title IX amendments in the US would ensure equal opportunities for women in college sport.

Leading the charge in 1970 was a group of nine women tennis players, who were not going to accept the status quo of women as second-class citizens in professional tennis. These women are called the Original 9.

Billie Jean King (twenty-seven), Jane 'Peaches' Bartkowicz (twenty-one), Rosie Casals (twenty-two), Judy Dalton (thirty-two), Julie Heldman (twenty-five), Nancy Richey (twenty-eight), Kerry Melville Reid (twenty-three), Kristy Pigeon (twenty) and Valerie Ziegenfuss (twenty-one) signed a contract on a $1 bill to kickstart the Virginia Slims Circuit in 1970. Gladys Heldman, Julie Heldman's mother, would help rope in Philip Morris as a sponsor. Back then, the tennis establishment had organized tournaments predominantly for men with some of the tournaments featuring women. Women's tennis was relegated to the outer courts, lower-prize money and women players didn't have even the basic support system.

Nancy Richey recollected, 'I knew tennis . . . take the subway . . . then take the subway back, the bags weighing 50 pounds more full of wet tennis clothes . . . No money, no lunchroom, nothing' (Fischer, 2018). Now (2018), the players are playing for millions, the women get equal prize money and the game has grown. I think it's absolutely fantastic.

'Every time I walk into Flushing Meadows I hug myself, because it's what we dreamed would happen in our game.'

The Original 9 were brave to break away and sign the $1 contract in 1970. They were not necessarily the nine best tennis players of their generation. Only two of them had won a Grand Slam—Billie Jean King and Nancy Richey. Their average age was only twenty-four. They were just starting out in their professional careers. Many tennis stars of that generation had stayed out of it, Chris Evert and Margaret Court amongst them. The Original 9 were taking huge risks, their careers could be over just as they were getting started. Rosie Casals,

Illustration 6.1: The Original 9 with Their $1 Contract

ranked third at that time and having reached the finals of the US Open twice, said:

'Jeopardizing the chance to play Grand Slams was probably the riskiest part of going against the old establishment . . . we were really second-class citizens . . . the Grand Slams were everything to us at that time. It wasn't just about money, it was about recognition, being given places to play and being paid fairly for something you did well.'

Kerry Melville Reid and Judy Dalton, the two Aussies in the Original 9, faced sanctions back home and couldn't play in tournaments as a direct result of having been Original 9 player signatories to the Virginia Slims Circuit deal. Kerry Melville Reid said:

> 'We had a strong leader in Billie Jean—she was a top player and she was powerful.'

Billie Jean King was twenty-seven in 1970 and was convinced that bold steps needed to be taken for the health of women's tennis. In this effort, she had the support and guidance of Gladys Heldman who had also helped her daughter Julie Heldman as she navigated the tennis world as a young female professional. Billie Jean King said:

> 'We knew that to really have a future, we had to have a tour, or a series of tournaments.'

The Original 9 faced significant uncertainties including being thrown out of the tennis establishment.

> 'We had no idea what was going to happen but we had the dream, the vision. We wanted every little girl in the world to have the opportunity to play and, if she was good enough, make a living from tennis.'

Five of the Original 9 came from California, a hotbed for feminism. Kristy Pigeon, the youngest of the Original 9, had just won the junior events in Wimbledon and at the US Open.

She looked back, saying:

> I went to schools in Oakland and Berkeley that promoted huge feminist attitudes . . . those true original feminists . . . they didn't make nearly as many waves as we tennis players did. We demonstrated that as sportspeople we were as interesting as the men. Our competition was stimulating to watch and could pull the people in.

> For me, that's a more powerful way of establishing equality.

Virginia Slims Circuit's performance would establish women's tennis and lead to the formation of the Women's Tennis Association (WTA) in 1973. By the end of that decade, there were more than 250 professionals affiliated to the WTA. Fifty years on, by 2020, the WTA had more than 2500 players from close to hundred countries playing in women's tennis tournaments, competing for $146 million in prize money. Twenty Indian women feature in the WTA rankings.

Claudio Ranieri and Leicester City 2015–16

Like any manager whose team faced the relegation dogfight, Claudio Ranieri maintained steadfastly, at the beginning of the 2015–16 PL (Premier League) season, that the main objective for Leicester City was to survive relegation. Since the inception of the PL in 1992, only five teams had ever won the PL—Manchester United, Chelsea, Arsenal, Manchester City and Blackburn Rovers.

> Leicester City, like any other team in the league, had a chance, of course, a slim chance of 1 in 5001, according to the bookmakers.

This season was different. Leicester City snatched the lead on match day number thirteen of the league and never fell below number two from thereon. From match day number twenty-two (out of a total of thirty-eight match days in the season) they remained in the lead. Eventually, they finished with 81 points, 10 more than second placed Arsenal. The squad employed by Claudio Ranieri through the season had been put together at a budget of only £50 million. Rich competing clubs like Manchester United, Manchester City and Chelsea bought and sold a single player for much more. When the PL was in the bag, they were now worth more than four times that!

So, yes, Leicester City's achievements weren't *because* of club wealth. Rather, they *created* club wealth.

Leicester was a 5000:1 underdog (Northcroft, 2016) with the bookmakers for good reason. They had climbed into the PL after winning the championship a couple of seasons back. In their first PL season, they had barely managed to hold on and avoid relegation.

Attention to each player's development was the hallmark of Claudio Ranieri's management.

Mahrez, the quick and relatively lightly built winger, came from Algeria. This was after Ranieri personally assuaged fears that the physical and fast football of the PL may hurt Mahrez. The Spanish league, La Liga, may have suited a fast and less physical player like Mahrez. But Steve Walsh, the Leicester scout and Claudio Ranieri figured differently. The left footed Mahrez would be allowed a largely attacking role on the right side. This accommodation was made possible by the acquisition of the Frenchman N'Golo Kante. Kante ran tirelessly all over the pitch, giving other players, like Mahrez, around him the cushion to weave their magic.

Marshalling the defence was goalkeeper Kasper Schmeichel, whose dad Peter Schmeichel had won five

PL titles for Manchester United, playing under Sir Alex Fergusson. Wes Morgan, Danny Simpson and Christian Fuchs marshalled the back with Robert Huth.

> Ranieri was able to set up Leicester City to play to their potential, accepting player limitations. After all, in the modern era, a player budget of £50 million can only buy this much of talent.

This required each player in the team to buy into the larger team philosophy of simply putting your head down and achieve much more on the soccer pitch than the price tag would suggest is possible. He promised pizzas for his team if they won a match. These were handmade pizzas, and team members participated in making the pizza. It was a show of affection for his players more than a material incentive.

Illustration 6.2: Andrea Bocelli Performing the Aria 'Let No One Sleep' at Leicester's King Power Stadium. Ranieri Quietens the Crowd.

> The pizzas were more about instilling humility in his players and bonding.

Like Kante, players had many years on their contract that buyers were willing to pay top price for. In the 2018 World Cup in Russia, the stature of the Leicester foxes would improve even further. Kante featured in France's second World Cup win. Mahrez pulled Algeria through qualifications into the showpiece event. Vardy featured for England after having scored the most goals in the 2015–16 PL season. Kasper Schmeichel guarded the goal for Denmark in Russia.

Unlike the American leagues, the PL follows a laissez-faire approach to teams' ability to garner playing resources. The rich teams, generally, tend to get richer and assemble stronger squads. An outcome is the concentration of league championships in a few clubs' hands. The top leagues of England, France, Italy, Spain and Germany, all share this 'winner-take-all' league profile. Blackburn Rovers had won the PL in its early days in the 1990s. Over time, this private league, owned jointly by the teams of that season, has become increasingly concentrated.

Ranieri would reiterate that he'd like to think of himself as 'thinker man' and not as 'tinker man', which the press, sometimes, criticized him for being.

Ranieri's trust, humility and service orientation is clear even in the Leicester City's King Power celebrations after winning the league title. Andrea Bocelli, an internationally acclaimed tenor, had offered to sing during the celebrations or as Bocelli puts it, '. . . sing for their big fiesta'.

Over the season, diverse people, many far removed from the soccer world, were beginning to take notice of this David–Goliath fight. Bocelli sang the aria *Nessun dorma*. It means, 'Let no one sleep'.

Leadership

'Leader' and 'manager' are terms that are, sometimes, used interchangeably, especially in business organizations. There are leaders who do not manage. They may inspire many followers, however, do no management of those who may be followers. Some political leaders belong to this category. Likewise, there are many managers who do a great job at ensuring all the policies of an organization are adhered to by its employees. Many of these managers may not have any followers or, indeed, may not even aspire to lead. Whereas a leader is an agent of change, a manager is more adept at maintaining status quo. In that sense, leaders and managers may even be conceptual antitheses of each other.

Great leaders achieve the extraordinary by inspiring people and enthusing them with a sense of common purpose and mission (Posner & Kouzes, 1988). Leadership is a process of an individual (the leader) influencing individuals to achieve common goals (Northouse, 2007). Individuals are able to influence others through the socially constructed idea of power. There are five sources of this influencing power—rewards, coercion, legitimacy, expertise and identification. Whereas reward power and coercive power are formally bestowed upon the manager by the organization, the last two—expert power and referent power—are the dimensions where great leaders shine through. Referent power is bestowed by followers on the leaders due to the admiration with which the leader is regarded.

Transformational leaders stimulate and inspire followers to achieve extraordinary results. They have a high referent power quotient amongst their followers. Transformational leaders enhance the leadership capacity of their followers by empowering followers to go ahead and develop as leaders themselves. So, transformational leaders not only benefit their organizations but also their followers, individually. They achieve this through four important channels. First, they provide inspirational motivation. Second, as role models, they exert idealized influence. Third, they provide intellectual stimulation. Fourth, they provide consideration to the development of the individual. Authentic leaders are, simply put, those who 'walk the talk'. Their actions reflect their stated values and beliefs. Their character is more important than style. An authentic leader is self-aware, cognizant of their strengths as well as weaknesses, and in touch with the effect they can have on those they lead. Authentic leaders are self-aware, are of strong moral and ethical values while being strongly committed to the organization. Authentic leaders are able to deliver for their organizations, in addition to top performance, a high degree of interpersonal trust and positive citizenship behaviour. A servant leader inverts the pyramid and seeks to empower each individual's development along with superior organizational performance. Servant leaders embrace the current resources at the organization's disposal and seek to enhance the value of each resource, while simultaneously delivering superior organizational performance. A servant leader is identified by three core characteristics—trust, humility and a commitment to the service of others.

Leadership in Action

Here, we discuss three important leadership styles/approaches—transformation, authentic and servant leadership. These approaches to leadership are examined in the careers of Gregg Popovich, Billie Jean King and Claudio Ranieri, respectively. We examine Popovich's transformational leadership of the Spurs over more than two decades, Billie Jean King's spearheading of the Original 9 and the WTA as well as Claudio Ranieri's leadership of the professional soccer club, Leicester City, over the 2015–16 season.

Gregg Popovich's Transformational Leadership

A hallmark of Popovich's career is his thorough preparation and detail orientation towards achieving his basketball philosophy. Key ingredients of this philosophy are seeking international talent markets, enormous work output and player growth not just as basketball professionals but as mature, empathetic and smart, young men. Popovich was amongst the first NBA people who realized the high-quality international talent out there. He saw in these international players qualities of hard work, humility and a strong team spirit. His clear preference for this player type for over two decades sends a clear message to all his players. Play for the team. Right from his early coaching days, he has managed to assemble teams that would be happy playing with each other and stick together for the long haul. When Spurs won the championships, this further solidified Popovich's reputation. Through these, Popovich has maintained high referent power— players look up to him as a coach, as a role model and a father figure.

Billie Jean King's Authentic Leadership

Billie Jean King wasn't just a top singles, doubles and mixed doubles tennis player. She was willing to risk a backlash from the establishment for the path she took. This path had a simple goal—women tennis players should be paid on par with the men. Women have the right to a professional tennis career on their own terms. Even today, fifty years on from the Original 9's actions in 1970, women's sport does not get the same support as men's sport. However, women's tennis under the WTA has progressed leaps and bounds. It now has tournaments with a cumulative prize money of almost $150 million, more than 2500 women tennis professionals from close to a hundred countries. To take the stand that Original 9 took back in 1970 required a firm moral compass. From 1970 to 1973 things would move quickly. The feminist wave had gotten hold of the tennis world. Under Billie Jean King's authentic leadership, the WTA was born. Even today, even in the developed countries, even in games like golf, women still face an un-level playing field.

Claudio Ranieri's Servant Leadership

Claudio Ranieri's leadership of Leicester to the PL crown is characterized by personal attention to each player on the squad, and the leader's care for his team characterized by offering pizzas. When Andrea Bocelli, the great tenor, was singing *Nessun dorma* a wave of the manager's hand was enough to quieten the celebrating Leicester crowd. In a great rendition by the tenor, one witnessed an entire football stadium singing the chorus for the aria. Much like the run of a 5000:1 underdog to the league title, a tenor holding a football stadium would be unforgettable for the many who witnessed it. Ranieri showed that simplicity, humility and service orientation could be used to produce great organizational results as well.

Leadership in Other Businesses

In the concluding section of this chapter, we will examine transformational, authentic and servant leaderships in the business world. We will discuss, briefly, the leaderships of Reed Hastings at Netflix from 1992, Warren Buffett at Berkshire Hathaway from the 1950s and Howard Schultz at Starbucks from the 1980s. They are discussed as transformational, authentic and servant leaders, respectively. Their approaches to leadership have strong commonalities with Gregg Popovich, Billie Jean King and Claudio Ranieri, respectively.

Transformational Leadership of Reed Hastings at Netflix

What started as a DVD mailing business in 1998 under Reed Hastings would eventually go on to be *the* television and movie streaming business. Not only was it a transformative business model, Hastings exhibited a transformational leadership. Formal performance reviews were eliminated. Employees were encouraged to make their own decisions as far as they were in the best interests of Netflix. This was much like how Gregg Popovich brought his own keen insights into the NBA—high-quality international talent, emphasis on team play and emphasis on hard work and practice. The encouragement Popovich gave to players to read and develop themselves as individuals is similar to how Hastings encouraged employees to think for themselves and make decisions in the best interests of Netflix.

Authentic Leadership of Warren Buffett at Berkshire Hathaway

Right from his starting out in the investments business, before 1960, Warren Buffett has been a strong 'fundamentals' person. Be it his personal life or his investments approach, he stuck to some basic principles—frills were eschewed, fundamentals were respected, the view was always long term and people who bought into the view of business whole-heartedly were developed. With more than fifty years of hindsight, this may appear too obvious. However, it is difficult to do in real time. Be it his faith in ability of Coca Cola to generate healthy cash flows or his faith in Goldman Sachs in the midst of the 2008 subprime market crash, Buffett has been steadfast in following and applying these core business principles. Buffett doesn't hand hold the companies in which Berkshire Hathaway is invested. Instead, business leaders are hand-picked with the confidence that they would run the businesses in a manner that would generate value. This strong conviction in basic principles is emblematic of authentic leaders. For Billie Jean King, the faith in women's tennis as well as the groundswell of feminist ideas in society prompted her to take the risk in 1970 with the Original 9. Soon thereafter, in 1973, the WTA would be formed and began to grow exponentially under King's leadership.

Servant Leadership of Howard Schulz at Starbucks

Howard Schulz's care and concern for Starbucks employees reflected in many key policies—performance rewards, options to earn Starbucks stock and tuition benefits. He understood that for Starbucks to succeed with its strategy of being 'the third place', hiring people who would gel was the key. Sure, Starbucks stores needed to be located a short walk away from offices and needed to stock the variety of coffees that would satisfy the palate. At the same time, the stores needed to be run by competent people with the right attitudes. It would always be more efficient to train up new hires that had most of the skill sets in place. He respected and supported diversity. It was well understood that to grow into a global, 'third place' behemoth, Starbucks would need to respond well to diversity. For Ranieri, the £50 million player budget could either be used to build a team used to playing in the rough and tumble of the PL or it could be used to build a team with a winning potential, which would need to develop ways of dealing with the physicality of the PL. Ranieri had chosen talent like Mahrez and Kante, confident that they could be trained to perform well in the PL. Schultz doubled Starbucks stores in quick time, fuelled by the initial public offering funds. Ranieri was, similarly, able to quadruple player valuations in just the one season he held the reins. Schultz began to make it possible to store employees to pursue college education through financing options. Ranieri paid careful attention to the development of each player. He also wanted common experiences over which the whole squad could bond— making pizzas or bringing a world-class tenor like Bocelli to their stadium. This genuine love for their people shines through in the servant leadership of Schultz and Ranieri alike.

Strategy cannot be separated from leadership. Students of strategy would do well to consider the strengths and weakness of their natural approach to leadership. Transformational, authentic and servant leadership approaches provide reference points around which an individual's leadership acumen may be consciously developed. Sports provide umpteen opportunities to observe individuals' leadership. Gregg

Popovich, Billie Jean King and Claudio Ranieri are great examples of transformational, authentic and servant leadership styles. It is important for developing managers and leaders to be conscious of the sort of leader they want to become.

7

Being Spot On Using Behavioural Strategy!

Something to be remembered on the golf course is that, ceteris paribus, one is much more likely to sink the par putt than the birdie putt. Even if you were Tiger Woods. Getting to strategy leadership demands a rational expertise and being good at it demands an awareness of rationality blind spots. Simply put, we aren't as rational as we may assume. Marketers exploit it, wealth managers make mistakes due to it and leaders struggle to get big decisions spot on!

Birdie Par and Service Speed Differentials

Over four rounds of a typical Professional Golf Association (PGA) Tournament, golfers play seventy-two holes, eighteen holes on each of the four days.

Fewer shots taken to complete the holes, better the score. However, popular golf conversations do not refer to this overall score as much as they refer to the score with respect to 'par'. Now, what is 'par'?

Each hole has designated number of strokes over which the hole ought to be completed, from tee to the hole. This designated number of shots to complete a hole is its 'par'. There are short holes where golfers can get from the tee to the green in a single drive. These would typically be par three holes. At top golf echelons, players would sink the putt in one or two attempts. There are long holes where golfers may, on average, require three shots to get onto the green. Fairways may be long or have turns, typically with hazards like water, trees and bunkers. These would be par five holes. A majority of holes would, of course, be par four.

Finish the hole in one shot less than 'par', it's a birdie (a score of −1). Finish the hole taking as many shots as the designated 'par', then, of course, it's a par (a score of 0). Finish the hole taking one shot more than 'par', then it's a bogie (a score of +1). Birdies are good, pars are acceptable and bogies are bad. A round has eighteen holes and a tournament has four rounds.

Jim Furyk, one of the best putters on the PGA Tour with seventeen PGA Tour tournament wins and third on the all-time prize winners list (over $71 million), said,

'Par putts just seem to be more critical because if you miss *you drop a shot* . . . if you miss a birdie putt, it doesn't seem to have the same effect.' (Schwarz, 2009)

Justin Leonard, winner of twelve PGA Tour events and with career prize checks worth over $33 million, agreed,

'When putting for birdie, you realize that, most of the time, it's *acceptable* to make par . . . for par, there's probably a greater sense of urgency, . . . you're willing to be more aggressive in order not to drop a shot. It makes sense.'

Golfers do better at putts for par than they do at putts for birdie. In 2011, Pope and Schweitzer wrote a paper in the American Economic Review lending solid, empirical proof (ESPN, n.d.). In the paper, 'Is Tiger Woods Loss Averse?' Pope and Schweitzer (2011) show how economic agents were loss averse rather than the utility maximisers as assumed in mainstream management. Employing rich data from the high stakes, high competition and high expertise world of the PGA Tour, the pros were robustly more successful at par putts than they were at birdie putts. This was after controlling for alternative plausible explanations offered by the neoclassicists for the 'birdie-par' differential. Like Woods, Furyk and Leonard had acceded, missing par putts was just not acceptable to whereas birdie putts were good to succeed at, nothing lost if it didn't go in. Anbarci et al. (2017) revisited loss aversion, a fundamental construct in behavioural economics' Prospect Theory, this time in the world of professional tennis. In their 2017 Journal of Applied Economics paper, they showed that professional players exerted more effort when they were slightly behind on the scores.

Illustration 7.1: Birdie Par Differential and Tiger Woods

Posing the question, 'Is Roger Federer more loss averse than Serena Williams?' (Anbarci et al., 2017) They went a step further to establish that women were less sensitive to loss–gain frames as compared to men.

Both golf and tennis are known for player entourages including former champions and psychological professionals. Nick Faldo, the storied golf veteran with more than thirty-nine tournament wins and more than $13 million in golf pay checks, worked with the sports psychologist Richard Coop. Coop's wards or clients include many top golf professionals like the Aussie Greg Norman and the American Payne Stewart (Davidson, 2017).

Coop perceived his work as identifying and eliminating psychological 'interferences' from his clients' performance. To him, golf performance was simply potential minus interferences. Fewer the interferences, better the performance on the golf course.

Hot Hand and SER

Daniel Kahneman, winner of the 2006 Nobel Prize in Economics, speaks fondly of the early years when he and his friend Amos Tversky collaborated on foundational behavioural economics work. In 1985, Gilovich, Vallone and Tversky (GVT; Gilovich et al., 1985) studied how fans of the Philadelphia 76ers perceived the success chances of a basketball shot, given the success or failure of previous shots. They found valid evidence in favour of fans 'seeing' streaks where there were none. Continuous shot successes could be possible due to inherent variations, given a shooter's overall success rate.

> If students at marquee educational institutions could succumb to the bias of seeing patterns where there aren't any, one would do well to guard against such cognitive aberrations.

GVT's 1985 paper found that when it came to field goal attempts of the Philadelphia 76ers, there was no positive correlation between successive field goal attempts. Neither was there a positive relationship between successive free throw attempts of the Boston Celtics.

> Controlled shooting experiments of the Cornell varsity men and women basketball teams yielded similar results—that there was no evidence of a shooting streak. However, they believed in the existence of the streak, though research didn't yield statistical evidence for a 'hot hand'.

The 'hot hand' was deeply entrenched in the thinking of the best basketball minds. In other sports as well, 'being in the zone' and 'flow' had been perceived as skills and coaching investments have been made to enhance these streaks.

In 2016, Green and Zwiebel (2018) revisited the hot hand. They argued that the hot hand may appear to be an illusion in sports like basketball characterized by Strategic Endogenous Response (SER).

That is, in basketball when a shooter is 'hot' the opposing coach would place more defensive resources against the 'hot' shooter. Therefore, Zwiebel and Green argued that shooting performance falls away, not because there is no hot hand, but because every subsequent shot attempted by the 'hot' shooter faces sterner defence. They turned their attention to sports which featured less SER. For example, once a bowler starts an over, there is little the fielding captain can do if the batswoman hit a couple of sixes. The bat and ball sport that Zwiebel and Green studied was baseball. They examined over twelve years of MLB data and over 2 million at-bats. They employed the previous twenty-five at-bats as the relevant, recent performance, given baseball's understanding of streakiness. They found that—over five batter and five pitcher metrics—there was indeed evidence of streakiness.

Zwiebel says, 'The earlier researchers were too quick to conclude that the belief in a hot hand was evidence of a cognitive or behavioural mistake. Most likely, what's really at work is not so much a mistake but an "equilibrium adjustment" around the hot-handed player—similar to the kinds of equilibrium adjustments that occur in finance and economics' (Andrews, 2014).

For over four decades, the conversation between rationalists and behaviourists over the hot hand had missed this important intervening, sporting detail— the SER.

> Hat-tricks in soccer or in cricket are celebrated because, in each sport, there is adequate opportunity for SER. For example, more defenders may mark an opponent attacker who just scored a brilliant goal, batters may consciously try to dig out the yorker rather than try to score runs facing a bowler 'on a hat-trick'.

A clear understanding of streaks is difficult even though they contribute significantly to individual and team performance. In a competitive milieu, thinking clearly of streaks is of paramount importance. How to keep a streak going? How to defend against a streak?

They Saw a Game

In 1951, Princeton and Dartmouth played a football (American football) game that was a bitter battle with both sides committing serious infringements and fouls so severe that at least one football player's college career ended. Professors Albert Hastorf of Dartmouth and Hadley Cantril of Princeton researched how students of Dartmouth and Princeton recollected the game based on each group's prior conviction that their university was great and could do no wrong.

In their 1954 paper 'They Saw a Game; A Case Study' Hastorf and Cantril (1954) examined the nature of belief formation. They found that Dartmouth (Princeton) print media and fans believed that Princeton (Dartmouth) had committed the more egregious offences and fouls.

In neoclassical approaches to studying decision-making, rationality was, at the time, the centrepiece. Humans form beliefs and update them on the basis of the evidence presented in front of them in a rational manner: that was the neoclassical assumption.

To the contrary, Hastorf and Cantril found that our beliefs determine what we see.

For the Dartmouth (Princeton) fans, their team was the victim of extensive fouls committed by Princeton (Dartmouth).

'We do not simply "react to" a happening . . . we behave according to what we bring to an occasion.' Our beliefs strongly influence how we process new information.

Dan Kahan, a leading researcher of biased reasoning revisited 'They Saw a Game' in 2012. This time, the paper was titled 'They Saw a Protest' (Kahan et al., 2012). Participants saw tapes of police halting a political demonstration. Employing video editing, some study participants were told that the political demonstration was against legalized abortion whereas others were told that the demonstration was against the (then) ban on openly gay and lesbian people's participation in the armed forces. What Kahan found was as follows.

> Based on the prior political positions of participants (when it came to legalized abortion and armed forces ban against gay and lesbian applicants), police (political demonstrator's) actions were justified and political demonstrator's (police) actions weren't justified.

An established belief is difficult to dislodge. Since most of us maintain the story of our life (Kahneman) and want this story to be positive and happy, evidence contrary to our storyline is met with 'motivated reasoning'. Motivated reasoning 'helps' maintain the current narrative, often through discrediting the sources of new information.

In 2012, psychologists Richard West, Russell Meserve and Keith Stanovich (2012) found that belief formation and questioning, both flawed in decision-making, didn't get better with the decision maker being more sophisticated with numbers!

> Cognitive blind spots prevented us from doing better with our beliefs and the more numerate subjects had *larger* cognitive blind spots.

That leaves us with three things to consider carefully. First, our beliefs are stubborn and influence how we see the world. The world we see doesn't smoothly update our beliefs. Second, when faced with evidence against how we see the world, we'd rather (for the most part) engage in motivated reasoning; discredit the source of new information than adjust our own bearings. Third, our ability to attenuate cognitive biases doesn't improve with being more numerate. In fact, being good with analysis and numbers may build our confidence in favour of the 'game' the way we have always played it. This hamstrings our ability to update beliefs because the more numerate and articulate amongst us could always interpret the numbers in favour of the status quo.

Behavioural Strategy in Action

Loss aversion, hot hand and stubborn beliefs all influence the way sports is played, coached and appreciated.

Loss Aversion

Pope and Schweitzer estimated that providing undue importance to whether a putt is being attempted for birdie (gain frame) or par (loss frame) costs PGA golfers one stroke in a typical tournament consisting of four rounds. While putting for a birdie on a downward sloping green, professionals prefer to under hit so that they can be assured of par, even if they missed the birdie putt. Over hitting the birdie putt could lead to facing a tough uphill putt for par. This is so because bogies hurt them more than birdies make them happy (psychologically). However, we know that a shot saved is important, and hence, each putt deserves an equal attention to success, psychological dynamics notwithstanding. Sports psychologists like Richard Coop call this interference detrimental to sports performance. Top golfers have high-quality psychologists helping them with their game because these interferences are costly. How much?

In 2019, a top five finish in a PGA Tournament secured Anirban Lahiri's PGA Tour card for the next season. Though Lahiri has wins in the European Tour, Asian Tour and India Tours, PGA Tournament wins put golfers in the highest professional golfing echelons. A golfer is a small business unit. Fixed costs of competing in tournaments are comparable across the tours. However, the PGA Tour is much more lucrative in terms of prize money as well as brand endorsement opportunities. Only a few shots make the difference between financial riches and losing the tour card. Most tournaments feature the entire field of players for the first two rounds (thirty-six holes). After this, the bottom half or bottom third of the field is 'cut'. Players who do not survive the 'cut' don't earn any tournament prize money. Of course, they lose the shot at making a deep run and securing their tour cards. Golfers who don't feature in rounds three and four offer lower value to brands that support them. Hence, dropping one shot in seventy-two, due to a psychological bias, interference is clearly unacceptable. Golfers employ coaches to help iron out weaknesses in specific aspects of their game. An example is coach Phil Kenyon's clients including champion golfers Rory Mcilroy, Justin Rose, Lee Westwood and Martin Kaymer.

Hot Hand

People in sports and those analysing sport just did not see eye to eye when it came to hot hands. The former firmly believed in it while the latter perceived it as a cognitive bias of humans. In thirty-five years of research on the hot hand, it appears that short run streaks do exist. Researchers are finally in agreement with longstanding sports intuition. Be it in basketball or in golf or in shooting, psychologists like Phil Kenyon work extensively with sports people to understand streaks, lengthen positive streaks and minimize performance interference. In India, shooting schools like Gagan Narang Foundation employ top shooters, coaches, psychologists to help develop the current generation of Indian shooting talent, including Elavenil Valarivan who won the World Junior World Cup 10 m air rifle event in 2019. In shooting, there is nothing a competitor could do to contain the opponent shooting streak. In soccer and basketball, the story is different.

Andre Agassi had picked up on an important 'tell' when he faced his great rival, Boris Becker. The 'tell' was that Boris Becker tended to stick his tongue out, pointing towards the direction of where he was going to serve. So, if Becker was serving at deuce and he was going to serve wide of the court, his tongue would point towards his left. If he was going to serve straight down the middle, his tongue would point towards his right. After having lost a majority of their first six matches, Agassi had picked up on this 'tell'. Subsequently, he won a significant majority of his matches against Becker. A key component of his record was superior performance while receiving the Becker service. But if Agassi were to pick the direction of the Becker serve regularly then it would become obvious to Becker and his coaching staff. So, the challenge, Agassi reveals, was to 'hide the fact that he could read the Becker service at will'. To do so, he would have to ensure that there were no streaks when it came to moving in the correct direction. Rather, he would have to use his 'tell' selectively in the big match moments only.

This is a good example of how the combination of hot hand and SER plays out in sports. In basketball, where it all started, coaches play a significant role in managing player and team streaks under high SER. Coaches can call timeouts and they make player substitutions. Coaches may employ both measures to interrupt scoring streaks of an opposing player. Conversely, they tend to allow the game to flow when their own players are on scoring streaks. A large number of these decisions are interspersed throughout a game of basketball. Sometimes, coaches like Pat Riley or Phil Jackson or Gregg Popovich may allow the game to flow even if it meant conceding early leads. That is done with the knowledge that time-outs and substitutions may have more strategic value later on in the game. Close competitions tend to get down to the wire. Allowing their players on court to deal with opponent scoring streaks was also a show of confidence.

Stubborn Beliefs (They Saw a Game)

As we saw in the context of the 1951 Princeton–Dartmouth college football game, fans are stubborn with their beliefs. Other sports stakeholders could have similarly large cognitive blind spots. Fans, press, team owners, selection committees, captains and coaches could all suffer from the stubbornness of their beliefs. Their finely developed sport and leadership understanding may actually increase their cognitive blind spots, not reduce them.

Beliefs held by the basketball ecosystem in the US—coaches, scouts, team owners, college coaches—had ensured the rookies entering the NBA draft were primarily US high school and college graduates. The high-quality NCAA competition tested basketball basics, professionalism and a player's mettle to make it in the big leagues. Players from other parts of the world were generally considered to not be in a position to survive and flourish in the physical NBA game. When good players emerged, they were only seen as exceptions. This was an instance of motivated reasoning to support incumbent, stubborn beliefs. The most cognitively sophisticated basketball minds weren't able to get past their cognitive blind spot—great NBA talent can only come from the US system.

Exceptional players emerged from other parts of the world, but they were only that—exceptions. Today, close to 20 per cent of NBA rookie drafts are European players. A handful of NBA coaches like Gregg Popovich and Phil Jackson could look at the European shores and make good player decisions. They benefited from drafting good players at reasonable rates when others weren't even looking in that direction. This resembles how the main sources of Indian cricket talent were for the longest time. Some captains of the pre-IPL era like Sourav Ganguly were able to cast a wider net when it came to Indian cricket talent. The result—a railway player M.S. Dhoni gets a look in.

Behavioural Strategy in Other Businesses

Loss aversion of consumers has been exploited widely by marketers, exploiting the FOMO—fear of missing out. In a well-known study, Kahneman and Tversky showed that simply by focusing the message on the loss or the win, people decided to avoid the loss rather than achieve the win, even when the expected value of all the alternatives was exactly the same.

Loss Aversion on Discounts

Marketers create this 'loss' alternative by generating a sense of urgency (displaying stock levels, limited time offers, highlighting others who may be shopping for the same item) and modulating discounts (contrasting discounted price and original price, offering limited time coupons). In negotiation situations, a strategist can use loss aversion to her advantage and should be mindful of the counterparty preying on her own loss aversion (Manola, 2019).

Hot Hand and Mutual Fund Investing

Investors make decisions with an underlying hot-hand assumption. They may think that a particular mutual fund that has been performing well in the recent past would continue to do so going forward. There are many instances of mutual funding investments growing remarkably on the heels of good fund returns. However, immediately thereafter, the fund's performance may or may not continue to be good. It is quite possible that while the fund's performance over a ten-year period is positive, the average returns to investors could be negative. This is because most of the investors came on board *after* a period of good fund performance, not before (Dell, 2013). In other words, investors believe the hot hand of the fund. Sure, there is significant skill and acumen in fund investment strategies. That said, past successes of the fund may not necessarily imply future successes of the fund, let alone sound returns to the investor. A high-quality fund manager may have left the firm. Or a reasonably good fund manager may have experienced results in the top section of his or her expectation. Simply put, the fund messages we hear on news media of past successes—they have an insidious effect on our reasoning.

Belief Perseverance and Marquee Societal Challenges

Belief persistence or belief perseverance can be experienced in the face of important policy issues facing us as businesses, nations and humanity itself. Once someone has adopted a belief, even ones based on weak evidence, they tend to get entrenched. Their belief persists or perseveres even in the face of scientific evidence to the contrary. These include beliefs on immigration (in the western, industrialized, developed-country context), climate change, death sentence, the influence of violence portrayed in media or the utility of lockdowns dealing with Covid-19, etc. Myriad studies on the positive effects of immigrants into developed economies do not necessarily change the views of those who believe that immigration negatively affects their country (and its culture, even). Part of the problem of a carbon-intensive industrial complex is the belief that climate change is a cooked-up concept. The influence on business leadership and strategy of these cognitive traps can well be imagined.

Strategists need to worry not only about the external and internal environment of the firm, they need to be self-critical of their own perspective. Henry Mintzberg in his classic five Ps for Strategy (Mintzberg, 1987) points out that strategy can be looked at as perspective, a process of forming and learning from perspective. Forming and learning from perspective requires us to be mindful of how we see things. Aldous Huxley said, 'When the doors of our perception are cleansed, we can see things as they truly are.' Of course, that is easier said than done. The fascinating world at the intersection of psychology and business is something all business leaders would do well to acclimatize themselves with.

8

Sorting Out the Network with Bosman Ruling and Resource Dependence Theory

We may neither be as inert to the world outside (as internal organization perspective assumes, Chapter 2) nor as powerless (as EE perspective assumes, Chapter 3). It becomes important to understand how this web, this network works. It's important to understand the spider and not become an insect in its web. Just think about how Brexit impacts university stakeholders, especially Indians, or how much influence Miramax had in the 1980s–90s or how intractable the administrative fight against the Covid-19 pandemic, sometimes, appears to be.

Bosman Ruling

In 1990, RFC Liege, the first division Belgian professional soccer club chose to not extend the contract for Jean Marc Bosman, then a twenty-five-year-old player (Brand, 2015). For a player to move from club A to club B, A and B needed to agree on the price B would pay A for the player. This applied to players who had a contract with A. Interestingly, it also applied to situations where the player's contract with A had lapsed. RFC Liege's investment in this particular player, Bosman, hadn't quite worked out well. Hence, when the two-year contract lapsed in 1990, Liege did not extend or renew their contract for Bosman.

> RFC Liege couldn't agree on a transfer price for Bosman with the French second division club Dunkirk. This was after Dunkirk was ready to give Bosman a contract.

Hence, Bosman's deal with Dunkirk fell through.

Bosman's salary at RFC Liege was cut by around 75 per cent. Rather than signing this new contract, Bosman sued Liege, Belgian Football Association and UEFA under the 1957 Treaty of Rome which gave labour like himself freedom of movement within the European Union (EU). Represented by lawyers Luc

Misson and Jean-Louis Dupont, a protracted legal battle ensued in the European Court of Justice.

In 1995, Bosman, who was now a thirty-year-old former professional soccer player, won the battle. It is now famous not only in football but even in basketball as the 'Bosman ruling'. The ruling was that a player could automatically leave the club on contract expiry.

> This changed things dramatically in favour of the player. When the player's current contract was close to expiring, the player could negotiate higher wage rates and signing bonuses with the buying club on account of being a free agent.

At around the same time, television-driven money reaching football coffers expanded significantly. European courts ruled against limitations on foreign players in the playing squad as well. Professional soccer leagues simply looked across national borders for the best players around whom strong soccer brands—players, teams and leagues—could be built. These dynamics driven by the Bosman ruling led to the transfer market for professional players taking off.

In the six seasons after the Bosman decision the world record transfer fee was broken eight times and moved from $20M to $70M. It had taken 20 years for the previous eight world transfer records and the high water mark moved from \$3M to \$20M.

(McMahon, 2015)

As of 2020, thirty-five soccer players have been transferred with a price tag of more than €100 million. In 2018, Neymar's transfer from Spanish giants Barcelona to the French capital's Paris Saint-Germain Football Club (PSG) cost the Parisians over €300 million.

Pre-1990, players moved on free transfers mainly because of injury, unfulfilled promise and as veterans. Bosman, you would recall, belonged to the second category. However, the Bosman ruling gave successful players a useful tool in the player market, 'free-agent' status. Free agent signings, also called Bosman transfers, included many successful players at the primes of their careers. Examples are Steve McManaman (Liverpool to Real Madrid in 1999, at twenty-seven), Sol Campbell (Tottenham Hotspur to Arsenal, at twenty-seven) and Robert Lewandowski (Borussia Dortmund to Bayern Munich in 2014, at twenty-six).

The player market involving the big European leagues has grown exponentially since the Bosman ruling. In the 2019 summer transfer window clubs of the big

> five leagues of Europe—the top divisions of England, France, Spain, Germany and Italy—completed 1932 deals worth cumulative of £5.25 billion! (McVeigh et al., 2019)

In 2003, Chelsea Football Club, founded in 1903, had a new owner—Roman Abramovich. The Russian billionaire infused huge cash into the club. One of the areas in which the cash was spent was in acquiring top-class coaching and player talent.

Player	Position	Transfer from and to Clubs	UK Pound Millions
João Felix	Forward	Benfica to Atlético Madrid	113.00
Antoine Griezmann	Forward	Atlético Madrid to Barcelona	107.60
Eden Hazard	Forward	Chelsea to Real Madrid	88.50
Harry Maguire	Defender	Leicester City to Manchester United	80.00
Nicolas Pépé	Winger	Lille to Arsenal	72.00
Romelu Lukaku	Forward	Manchester United to Inter	70.00
Lucas Hernandez	Defender	Atlético Madrid to Bayern Munich	68.00
Matthijs de Ligt	Defender	Ajax to Juventus	67.80
Frenkie de Jong	Midfielder	Ajax to Barcelona	65.30
Rodri	Midfielder	Atlético Madrid to Manchester City	62.60
João Cancelo	Defender	Juventus to Manchester City	60.00
Luka Jovic	Forward	Eintracht Frankfurt to Real Madrid	57.70
Tanguy Ndombele	Midfielder	Lyon to Tottenham Hotspur	55.50
			968.00

Table 8.1: Top 13 Player Transfers in the 2019 Summer Transfer
Source: Transfer Market. (2020). Top 13 player transfers in the 2019 summer transfer window of the Big-5 European leagues [E-Reader Version]. Retrieved 11 May 2020 from https://www.transfermarkt.com/

So much so that the scarce resource for rich clubs was open spots on the playing rosters. The rich clubs had far more players on their roles than the playing opportunities that could be extended to these talented players. At the same time, there were other clubs with serious footballing aspirations but humble financial means. Enter player loans.

Players could get loaned out to other clubs for a season or two. This allowed the richer clubs to still be able to control top-class player talent. An example is Thibaut Courtois. In 2011, Courtois joined Chelsea from Genk for a reported €9 million, five-year deal. He was nineteen. Of course, Chelsea already had a top-class goalkeeper in Petr Cech. In a move that made financial sense for Chelsea, career development sense for Courtois and a good player for the club with high aspirations—Diego Simeone's Atletico Madrid, Courtois went on a loan deal to the Spanish capital. After three successful seasons and establishing himself as a top goal tender at Atletico, Courtois returned to Chelsea in the 2014–15 season.

Thousands of soccer players criss-cross between clubs these days, all in search of a successful fit and financial rewards. A single stint at a top European club may only last two seasons on average, but free movement enables the players to have a fair shot at finding great success and a meaningful professional playing career.

Bosman achieved for football players what a Maradona or a Pele may have achieved on the pitch. Football players like other professionals could pursue what was in their best interests 'freely'.

Its effects haven't been restricted to professional European soccer alone. Across the pond, NCAA basketball players have benefited as well, if they have a citizenship or dual citizenship status in one of the EU countries.

In 2009, the University of Florida sophomore, Nick Calathes, left school early to play professional basketball. He headed not to the NBA but to the Greek professional basketball league. He utilized his dual US–Greece citizenship to sign a three-year, $2 million a year, deal with benefits. NCAA basketball coaches like the Florida Gators' Billy Donovan have had to deal with this added dynamic. Calathes returned to play for the Memphis Grizzlies of the NBA between 2013 and 2015. In 2015, Calathes returned to Panathinaikos (Greece), where he had started his professional career in 2009. In his case, the dual citizenship of an EU country opens, significantly, more professional opportunities.

JM—Superagent

Soccer, like any professional sport, is a lot more than the players featured on the field. The active players are simply the best configuration chosen by the manager or coach in a dynamic talent environment. Coaching staff continually deals with injury, loss of form, up and coming stars, players doing well in other clubs, prospects in traditional catchment areas, players on roll who may earn a good market price now, etc. Of these, the last four mentioned activities require the simultaneous examination of talent currently on the club's rolls and talent that is plying its trade elsewhere. Soccer being a truly global sport, talent could pop up from markets that the club didn't traditionally engage with. Soccer talent doesn't necessarily emanate from formal coaching centres only either.

> Eduardo Galeano, the Uruguayan poet and soccer lover, says that it is very tough for formally trained soccer minds to understand the South American player. After all, that would only come with knowing how it is to play soccer amid the squalor of the streets, on an empty stomach.

Galeano's insight may not hold as strongly today as it did back in 1982, when Boca Juniors of Argentina sold a twenty-one-year-old Diego Armando Maradona to Barcelona for $7.7 million. There were very few systems back then to help young football players integrate into Europe's football elite.

With the growing internalization of European soccer and increased player mobility grew the importance of 'agents'. Agents streamlined information flow in the player market and helped players acclimatize and outperform. The role performed by players' family was now being performed by formal player agents.

By 2020, soccer agents like JM's Gestifute represented many high-value and/or high-potential players as well as managers. They had come to occupy a central and critical position in the player transfer market.

By 2020, Gestifute was already involved in player transfers worth in the excess of $1 billion.

Almost all the managers JM represents are from Portugal. The most celebrated of these managers is, of course, Jose Mourinho, the fifty-seven-year-old wizard currently managing Tottenham Hotspur of the EPL. JM's contract with the Special One runs through to 2023. Portuguese club Benfica's manager Bruno Lage, English club Wolves' manager Nuno Espirito Santo and Italian giants Roma's manager Paulo Fonseca are all represented by JM as well (Transfermarket, n.d.). JM currently represents 120 professional soccer players, seventy-four of whom play for clubs all over Europe. JM representation is not for all players. Given the agent's own nationality and background, Portugal is an important catchment of the agent's soccer talent. Twenty-four of the forty-seven Portuguese players represented by JM play in Europe's big five leagues. That is an astonishing 50 per cent that play in one of five leagues—England, France, Spain, Germany or Italy. The average age of those playing in the big five is twenty-six. It includes top players like Manchester City's Bernardo Silva and Joao Cancelo, and Barcelona's Nelson Semedo. Those Portuguese players represented by JM and playing at home are younger—twenty-three. From amongst these, the successes will eventually move to one of the big five leagues. Some of these young players are Ruben Dias, the centre back who plays for Benfica, Miguel Luis, the central midfielder who plays for Sporting CP, and the goalkeeper Tiago Sa, who plays for Braga.

Gestifute's Portuguese players operating in one of the big five leagues command an average transfermarkt (see www.transfermarkt.com) valuation of about €17 million. Actual market figures are typically a multiple of two or three over this valuation. On the other hand, Gestifute's two Brazilian lads operating in England have an average valuation of €56 million. The three Argentineans operating in England, France and Spain have an average transfermarkt valuation of €17 million. That includes Angel Di Maria who plays for PSG of Paris.

So, JM's ability to identify and channel the best player talent to marquee leagues doesn't stop with Portugal alone.

JM has proven to be an astute talent spotter, negotiator and deal closer with an eye for clubs willing to pay for Band-Aid solutions to their squad problems. The Portuguese soccer club Famalicao was purchased in 2018 by Idan Ofer, the Israeli billionaire. JM was close at hand (Ronay, 2020). Famalicao, minnow and newcomer to the Primeira Liga, was able to buy players from the top European clubs. On the league table, they have managed to scrap with the more established Porto, Benfica and Sporting Lisbon. They appear to have a good chance to make it into the Champions League. Another club that has a good number of players represented by JM is EPL's Wolves. They have also benefited from the arrival of top Portuguese players. There is no prize for guessing who represents them—JM.

At the quick-fix end of the spectrum is the career of Renato Sanches, details of whose transfer are available in Table 8.2.

Sold as a nineteen-year-old to the German behemoths, Bayern Munich, for €35 million, Sanches' career may not have panned as hoped for. As the table shows though, that hasn't stopped him being transacted for more than €63 million within four years (2016–20). He was on loan from Bayern to Swansea for a season for a loan fee of €8.5 million. After that, in 2019, he was sold to Lille for 20 million. But JM's reputation was built on an earlier transfer in 2003 of a certain Cristiano Ronaldo from Sporting Lisbon to Manchester United.

Ronaldo's development into a soccer star has its roots in the six years he spent at Old Trafford under the watch of Sir Alex Fergusson. Table 8.3 shows the growth in his financial value from the age of eighteen (€19 million for Manchester United) to the age of twenty-four (€94 million for Real Madrid) and to the age of thirty-three (€117 million for Juventus). This growth in Ronaldo's value is, of course, concomitant with the great individual and team achievements on the pitch.

> Some players under JM's watch seem to rotate through the clubs with who JM appears to have a close working relationship. Each deal generates cash for the agent, signals market value of players, and continually adds to the strength of the superagent, JM.

But it is not all about individual, unrelated player transfers either. JM's deep relationships at Wolves (England), Famalicao (Portugal), Porto (Portugal) and Atletico (Spain) point to a pivotal role he plays in finding players/clubs for clubs/players. It involves a deep understanding of the requirements (pipeline) of multiple stakeholders. These may be in the form of information or in the form of trust. In the middle of all this is also a young soccer talent who wants to maximize his earnings' potential in the hyper-competitive, professional soccer.

Table 8.2: Renato Sanches (born: 1997)

Season	Date	Left		Joined		MV	Fee
19/20	Aug 23, 2019	Germany	Bayern Munich	France	LOSC Lille	€18.00m	€20.00m
17/18	Jun 30, 2018	England	Swansea	Germany	Bayern Munich	€20.00m	End of loan
17/18	Aug 31, 2017	Germany	Bayern Munich	England	Swansea	€22.00m	Loan fee: €8.50m
16/17	Jul 1, 2016	Portugal	Benfica	Germany	Bayern Munich	€20.00m	€35.00m
15/16	Oct 30, 2015	Portugal	Benfica B	Portugal	Benfica	€800Th.	-
15/16	Jul 1, 2015	Portugal	Benfica U19	Portugal	Benfica B	-	-
14/15	Jul 1, 2014	Portugal	Benfica U17	Portugal	Benfica U19	-	-
Dec-13	Jul 1, 2012	Portugal	Benfica U15	Portugal	Benfica U17	-	-
10-Nov	Jul 1, 2010	Portugal	Benfica Youth pounds	Benfica U15		-	-
				Total transfer fees :			€63.50m

Table 8.3: Cristiano Ronaldo (born: 1985)

Season	Date	Left		Joined		MV	Fee
18/19	Jul 10, 2018	Spain	Real Madrid	Italy	Juventus	€100.00m	€117.00m
09-Oct	Jul 1, 2009	England	Man Utd	Spain	Real Madrid	€60.00m	€94.00m
03-Apr	Aug 12, 2003	Portugal	Sporting CP	England	Man Utd	-	€19.00m
02-Mar	Jul 1, 2002	Portugal	Sporting U19	Portugal	Sporting CP	-	-
00/01	Jul 1, 2000	Portugal	Sporting Sub17	Portugal	Sporting U19	-	-
98/99	Jul 1, 1998	Portugal	Sporting Sub-15	Portugal	Sporting Sub17	-	-
97/98	Jul 1, 1997	Portugal	Nacional U15	Portugal	Sporting Sub-15	-	?
				Total transfer fees :			€230.00m

Resource Dependence Theory (RDT) In Action

In 1978, Salancik and Pfeffer's (1978) seminal work *External Control of Organizations: A Resource Dependence Perspective* (RDT) focused on how resources external to the firm could still have a strong influence on firm-level decisions. Between the polar opposites of total control over internal organization and lack of control over EE, there is also a relatively large sphere of influence of the strategist. This sphere of influence pertains to resources that may be external to the firm but over which firm actions have significant control and recoil. In their 1978 paper, Pfeffer and Salancik showed how managers of Israeli companies were willing to accept a lower return on their investments provided these were related to government-backed development. The more their companies depended on government work, the deeper discount they were willing to accept. Similarly, American defence contractors were willing to drive affirmative action policies for women in their workforce. The more they depended on the US Army work, greater was their voluntary compliance of women-at-work in their recruitment practices.

Over the next four decades, this stream of strategy has developed by paying attention to a wide variety of inter-organizational and intra-organizational relationships that have a significant effect on the firm's decision-making.

The Bosman ruling has greatly eased the movement of players across professional soccer clubs. By 2019, transfer fee spending of clubs of the big five European soccer leagues were over 6.6 billion (Lange, 2020). Thousands of players criss-cross across club and country boundaries bolstered by the pro free labour movement policies of the EU. Like Pfeffer and Salancik had conceptualized, clubs aren't stand-alone entities but part of a network where each organization aspires to acquire, develop, benefit and profit from the best soccer talent. Clubs, today, have to take a call on a young talent release or offer a long-term contract or offer a loan deal. Each of these relationships with a soccer player has its performance, player development, financial and strategic implications.

Let us reflect on the case of a thirteen-year-old Argentine player with some sort of a growth hormone deficiency arriving at the Spanish giant, Barcelona, back in 2000. It was possible that the prospect didn't develop the way many agents, scouts and soccer managers expected. In that case, a long-term contract could have hurt the club's finances badly. On the other hand, a short-term contract could have meant that just when Messi blossomed, another club—even maybe arch-rivals Real Madrid—splashed a huge deal and took him away from the New Camp to join the Bernabeu's *Galacticos*.

If not for Chelsea's new-found fortunes and zealously monopolizing young, soccer talent, Atletico Madrid may not have had the services of a world-class keeper like Thibaut Courtois with whom Diego Simeone's teams continued to punch way above their weight category. As it turned out, Chelsea loaned Courtois out to Atletico since they already had a world-class keeper, Petr Cech.

Soccer club managers, their agents, player agents, players, endorsing brands—all have to pay heed to this complex network. The network triggers player movements and player movements change the network dynamically.

Network Position Matters

More connected nodes of a network have more strategic information. The diversity of connected nodes determines the richness of the information available. Nodes in the player resource network may be players themselves, clubs and agents. While club management performs multiple activities, one of which is player transfers, agents have a singular focus on the needs of the clients they serve—both clubs and players. Agents may be oriented towards serving the needs of players and clubs as they come up, or they could be more proactive.

Agents like JM realize the high value of strategic information at their disposal. This information may be in terms of the quality of an up and coming talent relative to an already-established player. Were this information to be private, then it accords the agent significant wiggle room. By combining business acumen with high-value soccer knowledge, JM is able to make reasonably accurate estimates of how a young player like Ronaldo may develop going forward.

By working intensively with a few clubs, some in feeder countries like Brazil, some in EU stepping stones like Famalicao or Sporting, and some in the big five like Wolverhampton Wanderers (Wolves), JM is able to make good decisions at the switch. Some players like Ronaldo get the opportunity to grow into truly world-class talent at marquee clubs like Manchester United and Real Madrid. Should initial promise not convert into results on the pitch, then JM is able to engineer quick trades to increase the market valuation of players like Renato Sanches.

Whole Networks, Network Structure Matters

As conceptualized by Pfeffer and Salancik, the club as a node in the player transfer network is not entirely autonomous. At the same time, it is not entirely a slave either. Multidimensional influence and control can be achieved by a node (club) by strenuously striving to influence the whole network in which they find themselves. Clubs can drive stabilizing behaviours and strategies that attenuate the ebb and flow of player resources. Two key directions for clubs to take is towards trading with high-status partners and operating within closed-network structures.

Recently, strategic management scholars have attempted to do just that—to understand the whole network of players moving between clubs and how this network may constrain or enable clubs (Dhayanithy & Mukherjee, 2020).

Employing two decades of fine-grained data of player transfers in Europe, since its liberalization in 1995 (Bosman ruling), DM, 2019, identified something that would meet with the intuition of soccer followers—that there is an ebb and flow of transfers.

Given that the steep ebb and flow is costly for club management, it would behove strategists to look for ways to moderate the ebb and flow, have a smooth ebb and flow. Rather than having huge waves crash their shores, they would prefer for them to be gentler. The player transfer network in which the clubs find themselves embedded offers useful solution to the ebb and flow conundrum.

It turns out that clubs that have a higher status are able to control the ebb and flow better.

A club that transacts players with a larger number of counter parties is said to have higher status than a club that transacts players with fewer counter parties. Higher status is achieved by clubs transacting players with other clubs of high status. When Sporting sold Ronaldo to Manchester United, its status in the player transfer market rose because of United's status.

Clubs that operate in a network with more closure are also able to control the ebb and flow better.

For example, in 2017, Barcelona (Spain) sold Neymar to PSG (France), PSG sold the Frenchman Zagadou to Borussia Dortmund (Germany) and Borussia Dortmund sold Dembele to Barcelona. There is high closure involving the clubs Barcelona, PSG and Borussia Dortmund. With more closure, clubs are able to work with better information of counter parties and thereby anticipate future transfer scenarios better. This in turn allows them to control the ebb and flow better.

The flip side of this coin is that positions of high status and high closure in a transfer network may fence the organization off from novel, game-changing information somewhere out there in the network. Granovetter, in 1973, wrote an important paper in the *American Sociology Review* titled 'The Strength of Weak Ties' (Granovetter, 1983). Here, he discussed how, in the Chicago region, weak ties helped firms gain access to cheaper sources of fund borrowings. He found that firms whose CEOs were members of the same club as bank leadership managed to borrow funds at a cheaper rate. CEOs and bank leaders being members of the same club, sharing a round of golf or a game of squash, and maybe having a drink was nothing but a weak tie between the firm and the bank.

These weak ties gave firms access to novel market opportunities. Of course, a CEO whose network has high (low) closure may struggle to develop adequate weak (strong) ties.

The much-reported JM wedding of 2020 included Cristiano Ronaldo gifting him a Greek island! Now, that appears to be a strong tie. Over Cristiano's career, JM has brokered transfer deals worth €230 million. This requires the concerned parties to have a great deal of trust in one another. But a champion like Ronaldo doesn't come about too often. The year in, year out challenge facing professional clubs is the sourcing, trading and development of promising talent. Towards larger strategic objectives, clubs would do well to be cognizant of their position in the player transfer market. This includes not just outright transfers but loans, rights of first refusal, buybacks and cuts from onward transfer as well. Club managers ought to be cognizant of their emergent network positions. A deal that is very attractive (unattractive) may significantly erode (enhance) their network status and information opportunities.

For clubs like Famalicao and Sporting Lisbon, selling their players to big five destinations like Manchester United helps in building their reputation. For clubs like Borussia Dortmund, Barcelona and PSG trading players is easier because each counter party enjoys high status, thereby reducing risks. Even with super, high-quality players like Dembele and Neymar, a tough season can always happen. This is especially so in the rarefied heights of soccer competition like the Champions League.

While Pfeffer and Salancik looked within organizations for routines that may produce some stability, the whole network may itself be capable of delivering stabilizing benefits. Each transfer, dynamically, influences the network, which in turn influences the next transfer. It is obvious then that club strategists look beyond getting a player they need or selling a player for a certain valuation. They would do well to anticipate what a deal would do to the club's competitiveness on the transfer field as well as the impact it would have on future player valuations.

RDT in Other Businesses

Now, we will discuss wider business examples of external control of organizations, strategic implications of network positions and assessment of whole networks vis-à-vis an organization position in them.

External Control of Organizations—Brexit Impact on Universities, Academicians and Students

Just as the EU aegis allowed the Bosman ruling to transform mobility of players and brought with it attendant challenges for clubs, Brexit, voted in 2017 and negotiation window closed in 2019, transforms mobility of students, graduates and academicians. Challenges faced by British universities and its stakeholders are varied. Implications for aspiring students as well as for academicians are well worth considering.

Pre-Brexit, EU students were able to work in the UK after their graduation. This was not the case for Indian students. Indian students had a short window of three to four months to find a job after graduation or they had to return to India. EU graduates had the edge here. However, in new visa regulations that would come into force in 2020, Indian graduates would get two years post their graduation to find a job. This would be in line with the time all international graduates, including those from the EU, would have. This significant improvement in job opportunities is, perhaps, a key reason for a 42 per cent increase in Indian students seeking British universities for higher education (PTI, 2020). About 27,000 Indian students are registered in UK universities for higher studies. Similarly, the field may become more even for international candidates looking for academic and research positions in UK universities, relative to EU candidates.

Of course, British universities' budgets, especially research budgets, may fall. It remains to be seen how Brexit negotiations between UK and EU evolve. Policies governing exchange of valuable intellectual resources are bound to have a strong effect just as the Bosman ruling did on the valuation of these resources.

Network Position—Miramax (1990–2015)

In 2020, Harvey Weinstein was found guilty of rape in the third degree and a criminal sexual act and sentenced to twenty-three years in prison. In 2006, Tarana Burke, a sexual harassment survivor and activist, had used the phrase 'Me too' on social media. 'Me too' was a social justice and empowerment movement based upon breaking silence. It sought to 'empower women through empathy and solidarity through strength in numbers, especially young and vulnerable women, by visibly demonstrating how many women have survived sexual assault and harassment, especially in the workplace'. In 2017, Alyssa Milano posted #MeToo on her Twitter, relaunching the movement and bringing the pressure required to bring a long time, powerful and serial sexual offender like Harvey Weinstein to the law.

Harvey Weinstein's story points to how much power he had aggrandized in the industry. Between 1990 and 2015, a significant source of his power lay in Miramax, the company Harvey and Bob Weinstein had founded, producing great movies that brought critical acclaim and financial success. Overall, Miramax or the Weinstein Company, which they founded after they had to give up the Miramax brand as part of their separation with Disney, had produced or distributed 341 films that featured in Academy Award nominations (Oscars) and eighty-one which had won it (Berg, 2017). In the 1980s, Miramax was making its mark as an independent film producer of well, 'indies'.

Independent film producers offered a greater scope for filmmakers to stamp their vision on the movie, as compared to the large production houses like Universal. Indies were often screened in national and international film festivals before their mass market launch. They often tended to be small budget films, the successes among whom rivalled bigger movies of the large production houses. Many directors, actors, actresses and screenwriters saw their reputation enhanced greatly due to their work with Miramax.

Movies like *My Left Foot, Pulp Fiction, The English Patient, The Gangs of New York, Chocolat, Shakespeare in Love, Trainspotting, The Crying Game, The Piano, Rounders*—the list is endless—left a great impression on generations from the 1980s onwards. No other production house—either classic studios or independent studios—come close to the critical acclaim Miramax and Weinstein Brothers productions received.

Talent flocked to work with Miramax. At its helm, Harvey Weinstein wielded enormous influence in the industry and even with the Academy. His network position was that influential. Obviously, he abused this influence a great deal, too. It was a reputation to which a lot of the acting talent flocked, quite naturally.

What followed was decades of abuse. It could only be stopped by the courage of survivors who spoke up, the courage for somebody to say 'not on my watch' and the courage for somebody to say, 'MeToo'.

Whole Networks—COVID-19 Response

The theory of whole networks preceded our ability to represent and compute whole network measures. With the explosive growth of computing power that limitation has been released.

Whole networks can be seen everywhere. In 2020, with the outbreak of the Covid-19 pandemic, countries' responses have been varied. One common thread across all these responses is contact tracing. Contact tracing didn't start with the Covid-19 pandemic, of course. Just a couple of years back, with the successful control of the Nipah virus outbreak in Kerala, India is credited for the high-quality contact tracing that was carried out. In a virus outbreak scenario, contact tracing can help build a network of virus vectors. In a virus spread network, people who have met many people when they could infect others are high-status nodes. People who didn't travel to high-risk locations and who live in remote, sparsely populated locations are low-status nodes. When a new Covid infection positive case is identified, that family and, perhaps, that street and neighbourhood gain in status. Yes, in a virus outbreak, status is good for the virus to spread, is bad for the community that is defending against it. In addition to status, other whole network concepts like closure and bridging ties can help us visualize the virus spread better. In turn, this would help us developing better control strategies.

In this chapter, we discussed three sports cases that help us understand the world of strategy through the lens of RDT and networks. Bosman ruling, JM and the moderating effects of network structure—all set in the context of professional European soccer. Bosman ruling triggered unfettered transfer of soccer player talent leading to the creation of the network context for player transfers. JM's predominant position of superagent helps dominate the transfer market with astute connections to managers like Jose Mourinho, players like Cristiano Ronaldo and clubs like Famalicao and Wolverhampton Wanderers. In the volatile world of player transfers, some clubs can shield themselves better from the ebb and flow, thereby being much more cost competitive. RDT and network perspectives merit strategic understanding in other business contexts, too. These are as varied as Brexit's impact on Indian students who aspire to graduate from UK universities to what allowed Miramax to dominate the Oscars to how nations are looking to battle against the Covid-19 pandemic.

9

Battle of the Sexes

Sports is an amazing Petri dish to observe and understand how the 'dice is loaded' against women. Even in sports, where only the best elevate to the top echelons, there is still unequal treatment just on the basis of sex. 'My whole life has been about equal rights and opportunities. For me it really goes back to the health of mind, body and soul' (Stephanie, 2017). Of course, the battle of the sexes is ongoing in other walks of life and in industry. We call it different things. Just observe the lack of women in governance positions!

Player Wages for Indian Women's Cricket Team

In 2017, India won the Cricket World Cup (ODI) semi-final against Australia by 36 runs, powered by

Harmandeep Kaur, who finished 171 not out from 115 deliveries (strike rate 149 per cent). Out of 122 runs, 171 (71 per cent) were from hits to or over the boundary (ESPN, 2017). Another cricketer from the Hindi heartland—Kapil Dev, thirty-four years earlier, had launched an equally ferocious attack on the hapless Zimbabweans. His 175 not out took 138 deliveries (strike rate 127 per cent). Out of 100 runs, his 175 runs (57 per cent) were from hits to or over the boundary (ESPN, 1983). These were two great Indian innings remarkably similar to one another, including the margin by which India won—31 runs!

> But women's cricket in India couldn't be more different than the men's game.

Women cricketers Harmandeep Kaur, Smriti Mandhana and Poonam Yadav had, in 2020, a grade-A contract worth ₹50 lakhs a year (BCCI, 2020). Eight players have a grade-B contract worth ₹30 lakhs a year. Eleven women players had grade-C contracts, worth ₹10 lakhs a year. Pretty good remuneration, one would think, for women playing cricket—twenty-two women cricketers being professionally contracted by the BCCI to play for India. These contracts run through to October 2020. Despite the disruptions to the cricket season due to coronavirus, these professionals wouldn't be left in the lurch.

On the men's side, there is an extra grade—A+ (*Hindustan Times*, 2020). Under their A+ contracts, Virat Kohli, Rohit Sharma and Jasprit Bumrah would be paid ₹7 crore for the year 2020. Eleven Indian men's cricketers have a grade-A contract which pays them ₹5 crore this year. These players include Ravichandran Ashwin and Rishabh Pant. Only five players have a grade-B contract with the BCCI to play for India and it pays ₹3 crore a year. On grade-C contracts are eight men's players—youngsters like Navdeep Saini, Shardul Thakur and Washington Sundar. These contracts are worth ₹1 crore a year.

The twenty-two women Indian cricketers are contracted for a total of ₹5 crore and the twenty-seven Indian men cricketers are contracted for a total of ₹99 crore. The BCCI spends, in terms of player contracts, twenty times more (less) for the men's (women's) game.

This disparity between women and men at the highest levels of the nation's favourite pastime raises a serious issue, especially because these contracts provide opportunities for financial security directly and through brand and endorsement deals, mainly. Why would we, today, in 2020, have such a huge disparity between the sexes? Why would Harmandeep Kaur's contract as a grade-A women's BCCI cricketer be only half of say, grade-C men's contract holder, Washington Sundar.

In comparison, Cricket Australia (CA) is ages ahead. Since 2017, Aussie State women's and men's cricket teams get paid equally. Match fees for the women's national cricket league was made equal to the men. Women's Big Bash League prize money was whopping at more than $300,000. CA stepped in the top up of the Women's World Cup prize money for the Australian women's team since ICC events have an unequal pay structure.

> Also part of this policy was travel support, child care helper and a clause to allow pregnant players to don a non-playing role until they give birth. The board worked to ensure that their women cricketers are happy, to encourage more women to take up the sport. (Sankar, 2020)

This has gone hand in hand with the Aussies dominating women's cricket.

> While work on the awareness and popularity of women's cricket, central contracts and better facilities are starting to make a difference, 'We are five–six years behind them in these aspects,' said Harmandeep Kaur (ESPN, 2020).

In the hyper-competitive world of sports, competing on the field with a handicap of being five years behind on policy is severe. It may cause even expert cricket minds like former Indian skipper, Anjum Chopra, to take a narrow view on the issue of equal pay. 'I do not know why this has become a discussion point in such a big manner because we must remember that Indian women's team has never won a World Cup. Men's team has' (Jat, 2020). Interestingly, this was just after the Aussie women had beaten India in the 2020 T20 World Cup at the Melbourne Cricket Ground.

Challenges Facing Indian Women Shooters— Visibility and Respect

Indian women shooters have been making waves in the shooting ranges; seven of them earned Olympic quota places to represent India in Tokyo 2020. In the 10 m air rifle event, Anjum Moudgil and Apurvi Chandela will represent India in the Tokyo Olympics. Moudgil won silver in the 2018 World Championships held in Changwon, South Korea. Though Chandela finished fourth in that same event, she has been in great form since and had become top-ranked in the world in her discipline. In the 25 m air pistol event, veteran Rahi Sarnobat (Asian Games and International Shooting Sport Federation Munich World Cup Gold) and youngster Chinki Yadav (Asian Shooting Championships Gold) made their way to Tokyo. In the 10 m air pistol event, seventeen-year-old Manu Bhaker (multiple Golds and World Champion) and twenty-two-year-old Yeshaswini Deswal (World Cup Gold) qualified with aplomb. The seventh woman shooter to qualify was Tejaswini Sawant in the gruelling 50 m 3-position (3P) event (Commonwealth Games Gold).

> Despite the stellar performances in the world stage, these woman shooters may go unrecognized and invisible. This has been the lot of many talented sportswomen around the world and in different sports. Even when they gain media visibility that their sporting performances deserve, way too often, it is accompanied by the adjective 'hot'.

Media coverage of women's sports has become more sexist in the recent past. In 2004, Sepp Blatter asked female footballers to play in more 'feminine clothing' and bring 'aesthetic' value to the beautiful game. He was indicating that they take the cue from women's volleyball and went as far as to suggest they play in 'tighter shorts' (Ray, 2016).

> Coming from the most powerful person in soccer, then it was a point of view that reduced top athletes like Mia Hamm and Hope Solo to the glamour they could bring to the game. World over, many high-achieving female athletes have faced this sexist onslaught.

A great heptathlete like the British Jessica Ennis-Hill garners media coverage not only on her sporting achievements but 'her looks, model poses and domestic relationships' (Mansfield et al., 2017). The Aussie surfer Alana Blanchard may not have made it to the top 30 surfers list in 2016 but was one of the highest earning via endorsements and sponsorships—again based on certain heterosexual, white, male aesthetic definitions. Allyson Felix, the American sprinter, has won medals galore at the Olympics and World Championships and is one of the greats in her events—100 m, 200 m, 300 m and 400 m relays.

> According to her, the greatest challenge facing female athletes is 'visibility and respect'.

Gaby Douglas and Simone Biles are star gymnasts from the US who have won multiple Olympics and World Championships titles. Even after having some gymnastics skills like the Biles named after her:

> Biles faces comments and criticism of her being too muscular to be a world-class gymnast. These remarks are rooted in backward-thinking notions of what a woman gymnast ought to look like. Douglas and Biles have come out clearly against the body shaming they have had to endure to reach the pinnacle of their athletic careers.

For young Indian shooters like Apurvi Chandela and Manu Bhaker, it is very likely to be a challenge to gain the visibility and respect that they so richly deserve. In their sport—shooting, the competition is very internal, almost monkish. There are very few arenas in our country where shooting takes place in a computerized range and can be followed by a live audience. These constraints only add to the difficulty they would face to gain visibility. On the other hand, unlike volleyball or gymnastics or surfing, shooters wear full length, heavy clothing designed to regulate the body movement of the shooter and improve shooting precision. As a sport, it doesn't lend itself to objectifying the woman. That would hardly be any consolation if the shooters didn't get the visibility and respect for their great shooting performances on the world stage.

Women in Sports Governance

Of the seventy-four Indian athletes who earned Olympic quota places to Tokyo 2020, thirty-two were women (43 per cent). However, in the realms of sports administration and governance, there is scant gender diversity.

Hockey India features 34 per cent female participation in the governing body of the sports association. In all other sports bodies in India, there is only a 2–8 per cent representation of women (Sapatwala, 2020).

Writing on sport governance in 2017, Ian O'Boyle presented some telling data regarding women in sport governance (Bradbury & O'Boyle, 2017).

The IOC (International Olympic Committee) Executive Board comprised fifteen members with only four women (Bradbury & O'Boyle, 2017, p. 149). Of the 115 members of the IOC, less than a fourth were female. National Olympic Committees (NOC) had fewer than 20 per cent women in their governing bodies.

Even in developed countries like Australia, women participated and won medals on par or better than the men. In 2012 London Olympics, Aussie women won more medals than the men. However, when it came to their participation in sports governance, the story was different.

Between the Australian Olympic Committee and Commonwealth Games Association, little over 20 per cent of the thirty-four board seats were occupied by women.

In 2013, Australian Sports Commission (ASC) had set the target of a minimum of 40 per cent women in NOC boards. Reporting on gender representation on boards has also been made mandatory in Australia.

In India, the president of the Tamil Nadu Cricket
Association (TNCA), in 2020, was Rupa Gopinath,
who was a national golf player and the daughter
of the former TNCA supremo, N. Srinivasan. The
remaining fifteen members of the Apex Council are
all men. Karnataka State Cricket Association has only
two women on its board. Gayathri K.R. and Varsini
Arun, the women on the board were nominated by
the Indian Cricketers Association and the auditor
general, respectively. Of the sixteen office bearers and
councillors of the Mumbai Cricket Association, there
is only one woman, Samantha Lobatto.

> In the three regional powerhouses of Indian cricket—
> Tamil Nadu, Karnataka and Mumbai—only four out
> of forty-nine governance positions are held by women,
> a paltry 6 per cent.

Even in these relatively progressive parts of India,
it turns out that women are absent in cricket
governance and most of those present find place in
nominated, and not elected, positions. Barriers to
the advancement of women into sports governance
are many. They include attitudes and perceptions of
the 'male dominated' sport culture, perceptions and
expectations of (and from) women, issues related to
work-life challenges faced by women, and dearth of
opportunities for women at more grassroots levels.

Across countries and over time, it appears that the steeper these challenges, the more acute the dearth of women is in the management and governance of sport. While women appear to be able to surmount challenges to participate in sports and turn out to be champions, continuing to make contributions in the management and governance of sport appears to remain male bastions still. The ASC named and shamed all the agencies which were ASC funded but had fewer than 20 per cent of governance positions occupied by women. In the case of Basketball Australia, the ASC mandatory principles did lead to a significant overhaul in the way that sports organization was organized and operated, thereby leading to a significant representation of women in governance positions. Sports governance is one 'battle of sexes' that women are, and society is, yet to draw level at.

Battle of the Sexes—Pay Parity, Visibility and Respect, Governance Role

Women face three important and interrelated challenges as they craft their careers. These are to do with getting significantly lesser pay than their male counterparts, the continuing difficulty in gaining visibility and respect, and, ultimately, the disappearance of women when it comes to the governance echelons in sports.

Pay Parity

In 2020, to a $1 earned by a man, a woman would earn $0.81—adjusted for the type of job, productivity, skill and experience of the employee, and other relevant factors (Payscale.com, 2020). Equal Pay Day (EPD) is that specific day in the current calendar year that a women needs to work till she equals the earnings of a man in the previous calendar year. The closer (farther) EPD is to (from) 31 December of the base year (2019), the (weaker) greater is the gender pay parity. In the US, in 2019, compared to each $1 earned by a white, non-Hispanic man, on average, an Asian-American woman earned $0.85 (EPD 5 March), an African and Black American woman earned $0.61 (EPD 22 August), and a native American woman earned $0.58 (EPD 23 September). White women were paid better than women of other ethnicities. Across the US and Europe, various 'equal pay for equal work' laws have, for a long time, aspired to make it illegal 'to pay men and women different wage rates for equal work on jobs that require equal skill, effort, and responsibility, and are performed under similar working conditions.' Arguments abound in favour of 'equal pay for equal value'. Unlike equal pay, pay equity 'compares the value and pay of different jobs, such as nurse and electrician'.

Now, there may be various societal reasons why women do certain jobs and men do others.

Within a sport, however, gender role differences-based arguments to explain away pay disparity are difficult to maintain. Across sports, there are significant variations in how male and female athletes are paid. Tennis, especially at the Grand Slams, has moved purposefully towards paying the women on par with the men. Other sports like soccer haven't done such a great job. The 2019–20 plaint by US Women's soccer against the difference in the payments for male and female soccer players was denied by the US Supreme Court. This was on account of the pay structure having emerged from a collective bargaining agreement. However, the courts have been positive towards other aspects of the employment rights of women players. These include vacation, maternity leave, comparable travel and stay, etc.

While the US women soccer and women golfers continue to wage the battle for being treated on par with the men, it might well be a long-drawn battle fought just as much in the courts of public opinion as the legal courts. Figure 9.1 presents the pay (dis) parity between top men and women athletes. This comparison is useful because these athletes have all reached the pinnacle in their sport. There have even been seasons where Serena Williams has earned more prize money than Roger Federer! However, other huge earnings streams—endorsement and sponsorship deals, appearance fees, etc.—are stacked against the woman.

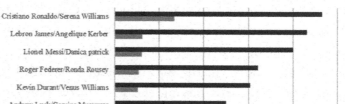

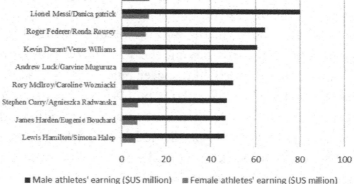

Figure 9.1: Forbes 2017 Comparison of the Earnings of the Highest-
paid Men and Women Athletes in Different Sports
Source: Forbes. (2017). Forbes 2017 comparison of the earnings
of the highest paid men and women athletes in different sports
[E-Reader Version].
Retrieved 3 June 2020 from https://en.wikipedia.org/wiki/Gender_
pay_gap_ in_sports#/media/File:The_income_of_the_top_10_highest-
paid_female_and_male_athletes_based_on_the_statistics_released_
by_Forbes_in_2017.png

In other industries' experience, skill and efficiency are,
often, explained as drivers for unequal pay. In sports,
especially between champion athletes, these arguments
aren't tenable. Therefore, there is a scope to help us
peep into the 'real' reasons behind pay parity still being
a dream.

Visibility and Respect

As recently as in 2019, Allyson Felix, multiple World and Olympic sprint and relays champion was quoted,

> Women are still not given the same opportunities as men, and it does not seem like our accomplishments are viewed as being as impressive as men's are. Unfortunately, over my career, I have not seen this change much. These issues have impacted every aspect of my career. They impact the economics of my business . . . (Portsche, 2019)

Allyson Felix won nine medals in the Olympics (from 2004 Athens to 2016 Rio) for the US, making her the most-decorated female athlete in the history of that country's track and field.

In a survey of 1800 people, it was found that men and women were believed to be equals in math and science. Unfortunately, '. . . many people agreed that in sports, both genders are definitely not treated equal.' Even more telling was the fact that 47 per cent of the women surveyed agreed that men were better (at the sport) and got more acknowledgement (for playing the sport). This is, of course, the line of thinking of the Indian women's cricket great, Anjum Chopra, who said, 'I do not know why this (pay parity) has become a discussion point in such a big manner because we must remember that Indian women's team has never won a World Cup. Men's team has.' It is heartening though that other female athletics stars take a more pro-active approach. Rather than viewing pay parity as contingent on great performance, it is seen as an enabler of the same.

Women in Sports Governance

Partly due to the afore-mentioned reasons, we find few women in sports governance. This deprives sports organizations of the representation which would enable organizations to deal with the battle of the sexes fairly. It also deprives organizations of the much-needed diversity, which has been unequivocally linked to sustained organizational performance. In their 2018 paper titled 'Women and Leadership: Advancing Gender Equity Policies in Sport Leadership through Governance', Popi Sotiriadou and Donna de Haan interviewed members of the Triathlon board of the international and two national federations (Sotiriadou & Haan, 2019). They found that effective equity champions challenged existing stereotypes at individual (micro), board (meso) and sport (macro) level. Equity champions enabled women to feel valued in leadership roles and could promote women in sports governance. But not every sports organization finds its equity champion.

As a result, women continue to be invisible in sports governance. In turn, this may lead to policy blindness to the specific and justified needs of women in the organization, as well as the needs of the organization itself. Ultimately, this denies female athletes the basics like pay parity, their visibility internal to the organization as well as broadly in society and, ultimately, their acceptance as sportswomen.

Battle of the Sexes in Other Businesses

Women face major obstacles vis-à-vis the men in all walks of life, hence, 'battle of the sexes' is used here in an indicative and not literal sense. Pay parity, visibility and respect and governance role are three important and interrelated challenges facing women across industries. The lack of gender diversity is a challenge to governance itself. The following section deals with the obstacles facing women in other business contexts and industries as well.

Pay Parity

Even amongst those who have a college degree in the US, the uncontrolled gender pay gap is significant (please see Figure 9.2). The controlled pay gap tends to be lower because of the various other moving parts in the determination of wages—educational level, experience, skill, etc., are equalized and then, the average pay of men is compared to the average pay of women. The gender pay gap in India stood at 19 per cent, women earned ₹81 for every ₹100 earned by men (PTI, 2019a). In a 2019 survey, it was found that men earned 26 per cent, 24 per cent and 21 per cent more in IT/ITeS, manufacturing and healthcare, and caring services, respectively. In financial services, women and men were paid, more or less, at par. While gender pay gap is at its lowest when men and women join organizations, it reaches its peak about ten years into one's career. There has, also, been hardly any reduction in the gender pay gap in recent times.

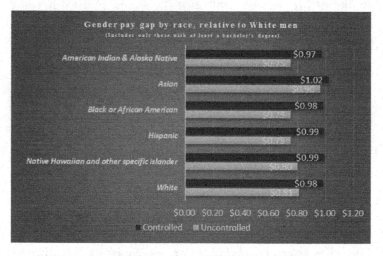

Figure 9.2: Gender Pay Gap 2020 in the United States
Source: Payscale.com. (2020). Gender pay gap 2020 in the United States [E-Reader Version]. Retrieved 3 June 2020 from https://www.payscale.com/ data/gender-pay-gap

Around 70 per cent of women and men surveyed in Indian corporates agreed that gender pay parity ought to be a top organizational concern. There appears to be a rather sticky perception that women are less serious about their work and career as compared to the men. This is seen to have a strong impact on women around the time of childbirth and with respect to the amount of time women are seen as putting in at work.

Visibility and Respect

In the previous section of pay parity, it had been discussed how female athletes are stymied in terms of media exposure and, therefore, constrained in their earnings and, indeed, career growth into governance levels. Around equal number of young women and men join the top IT companies in India from their undergraduate engineering colleges. In 2018, India dominated the number of H-1B visas awarded by the US. These employment visas typically allow IT professionals to work closely with their clients—across American industries—and thereby move towards higher-value IT profiles, from coding to project management. In 2018, of the more than 420,000 foreign nationals working in the US more than three-fourths were from India.

Of the countries on the top of the US H-1B visa list, India had the most-skewed gender ratio (Bhattacharya, 2018).

The *Monster Salary Index* publication (Monster India.com, 2017) indicated that 51 per cent of entry-level recruits in the industry were women, 25 per

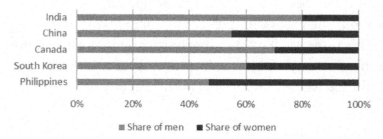

Figure 9.3: Gender Disparity in Indian H1B Visa Recipients
Source: Bhattacharya, A. (2018). Gender disparity in
Indian H1B Visa recipients [E-Reader Version]. Retrieved
19 June 2020 from https://qz.com/india/1431506/ most-h-1b-visa-
holders-are-indian-men-despite-donald-trump/

cent in managerial positions were women and 1 per cent in C-suite positions were women—all as of 2017 (Gupta, 2020). Now, this dropping off of women in the country's most international industry could be put down to internal reasons pertaining to management and governance of companies in the sector, or they could be due to external reasons pertaining, perhaps, to a patriarchal society that places limitations and constraints on what women should aspire for. Either way, IT-sector behemoths like Infosys, TCS, Wipro, HCL, Accenture, etc., are faced with a serious talent attrition problem. 'By 2011, HCL, Wipro and Infosys had about one-fourth to one third women in the workforce, but few in leadership positions. At Infosys, for instance, only 4.8 per cent were at senior management level' (Buddhapriya, 2013). Studies have found that despite there being more or less equal entrance of men and women into the IT sector, after eight years non-technical roles like testing are dominated by women (about 2:1), whereas technical roles like programming are dominated by men (about 2:1; Gupta, 2019). This is quite alarming given that 40 per cent of the graduates in computers-related areas are women. India's IT organizations may be facing a huge, gendered, talent attrition problem. While industry leading organizations continue to do a great job in sourcing talent in a gender equitable manner, it might be quite another story when it comes to a woman's ability to develop her career in the sector.

Women in Governance

Diversity on boards is good for competitiveness of a business organization. 'NASSCOM points out that corporations with at least 10 per cent women on company boards have 2.5–5 per cent higher returns on equity, firms where women are at least 30 per cent of C-Suite have 15 per cent higher profitability than others' (Raghuram et al., 2017). Having said that, there are still very few women on corporate boards of India. The Companies Act of 2013 mandated that there be at least one woman director. In the seven years since, directorships held by women had increased from 5 per cent to 15 per cent of the board (in 2019; Bhatia & Bhattacharya, 2020).

But there is a catch. 60 per cent of the Nifty 500 firms have just one-woman member on their boards and 30 per cent have just two women on their boards. In short, at this level of representation, women can be easily sidelined and may not be able to drive women-friendly policies in their respective organizations. In 2020, only three firms had equal representation on their boards: Apollo Hospitals Enterprise Ltd (five men and five women directors), Crisil Ltd (four men, four women) and Vinati Organics Ltd (three men, three women). Perhaps, it is not a coincidence that the managing directors in all three firms are women. Gender imbalance across top positions continued to be high. By 2019, 95.3 per cent of CEO/MD and 94.8 per cent of chief finance officer/director finance were men. Close to 20 per cent of independent directors on the board were women, indicating that while, sometimes, women had a seat at the table, it wasn't anywhere near the head of the table. Firm appear to be more comfortable appointing women as independent directors.

While the representation of women on Indian boards is higher than emerging market peers, it was significantly less than Organization for Economic Co-operation and Development countries. In fact, some developing economies like Turkey and South Africa feature more women on their corporate boards.

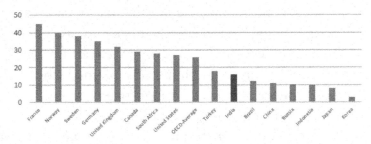

Figure 9.4: Women in Corporate Boards in Different Countries
Source: OECD. (2019). Women's representation on boards in India
is lower than OECD average, higher than EM peers.
[E-Reader Version].
Retrieved 3 July 2020 from https://www.livemint.com/companies/
news/more-women-are-joining-corporate-boards-but-very-few-get-
the-corneroffice-11583133282585.html

Figure 9.4 compares women representation on corporate boards across different countries.

Be it sports or in business, going from a young, high performer to the board involves access to opportunities and guidance. It is clear from the foregoing discussions that there is still a large chasm for women to cross before they can hold their own in this ultimate 'battle of the sexes'.

This is a great challenge facing not just the women looking to shatter the glass ceiling. Organizational leaders and managers face it and so does society as a whole. Irene Charnley started her career working in the National Union of Mineworkers, negotiating better pension and provident fund agreements with corporate leaders. She saw herself being able to serve the union and post-apartheid South African cause the best by employing her financial acumen and savvy. The Mineworkers Pension Fund would deliver financial security for hundreds of thousands of mineworkers and their children. It would go on to invest in many South African companies, including Johnic. At this point, Charnley went from union negotiator and financial advisor to the boardrooms of corporate South Africa. Charnley points out the progressive culture of the unions where she began her career, after returning from studies in London. In the unions, they used to address her as 'brother'—somebody who stood and fought with them side by side. It is a spirit where more organizations can benefit from greatly—be they sports organizations or corporate.

Acknowledgements

I have a number of people to thank for helping me get across the line with this manuscript. Professor Debashis Chatterjee's encouragement through the project has been constant and his guidance valuable.

IIMK faculty colleagues, MBA and doctoral students and IIMK alumni have, over the last decade, kept my interest in sports well fuelled. Be the casual, coffee kiosk conversations or classroom interactions or more serious research work, I have much to thank the IIMK ecosystem for. Right from the strategic management area discussions to larger formal interactions, ideas of various faculty colleagues have been invaluable.

Professor Deepa Sethi and Professor Rachappa Shette have been remarkably supportive and encouraging teammates. Sharing notes with them through the process of getting our respective manuscripts ready for the book series has helped me a great deal in the writing process. They and Professor Debashis Chatterjee, the series editor, often reminded me that all we needed to do was write consistently, break it down into small intervals and take encouragement from small wins.

Ms Rachna Gupta's support has been instrumental in navigating through the publication process. Ms Radhika Marwah is the silent force in my project. Her inputs were instrumental in structuring my thoughts in the form and shape taken by the manuscript. Satwik created six wonderful illustrations for the book and I thank him for his creativity. My academic associate, Devaki J., managed relatively quick turnarounds and helped improve the manuscript from the initial versions. I thank her for her diligence.

The Covid-19 pandemic broke in our part of the world just as this project started in earnest. Many people have had to face remarkable hardships and tragic losses. Mahesh Jena covered a distance of about 1700 km, half of the Tour de France, in his rickety old cycle from Maharashtra to Orissa, just to get back home. Right from April 2020, some of my friends and colleagues worked through trying separations from their families. Their equanimity in these times helped in maintaining a reasonably healthy perspective.

Thanks to my family for all the support, encouragement and inspiration.

References

Acosta, R. V., & Carpenter, L. (2005). *Title IX*. Human Kinetics.

Anand, V. (2019). *Mind master*. Hachette Book Publishing India Pvt Ltd.

Anbarci, N., Arin, K. P., Okten, C., & Zenker, C. (2017). Is Roger Federer more loss averse than Serena Williams? *Applied Economics*, *49*(35), 3546–59.

Andreato, L. V., Franchini, E., De Moraes, S. M., Pastório, J. J., Da Silva, D. F., Esteves, J. V., & Branco, B. H. (2013). Physiological and technical-tactical analysis in Brazilian jiu-jitsu competition. *Asian Journal of Sports Medicine*, *4*(2), 137.

Andrews, E. L. (2014). *Jeffrey Zwiebel: Why the 'hot hand' may be real after all* [e-reader version]. https://www.gsb.stanford.edu/insights/jeffrey-zwiebel-why-hot-hand-may-be-real-after-all

Argyris, C. (1977). Double loop learning in organizations. *Harvard Business Review*, *55*(5), 115–25.

Barney, J. (1991). Firm resources and sustained competitive advantage. *Journal of Management*, *17*(1), 99–120.

Baron, E. (2015). *Deans' salaries at top public B-schools* [e-reader version]. https://poetsandquants.com/2015/05/26/deans-salaries-at-top-public-b-schools/

BCCI. (2020). *BCCI announces annual player retainership 2019–20—Team India (Senior Women)* [e-reader version]. https://www.bcci.tv/articles/2020/news/144226/bcciannounces-annual-player-retainership-2019-20-team-india-senior-women-

Berg, M. (2017). *After expulsion from the academy, here are all of Harvey Weinstein's 81 Oscar wins* [e-reader version]. https://www.forbes.com/sites/maddieberg/2017/10/13/here-are-all-of-harvey-weinsteins-oscar-wins/#1d7cb155d946

Bhatia, S., & Bhattacharya, P. (2020). *More women are joining corporate boards but very few get the corner office* [e-reader version]. https://www.livemint.com/companies/news/more-women-are-joining-corporate-boards-but-very-fewget-the-corner-office-11583133282585.html

Bhattacharya, A. (2018). *What visa woes? Indians are still hogging most H-1Bs* [e-reader version]. https://qz.com/india/1431506/most-h-1b-visa-holders-are-indian-mendespite-donald-trump/

Bradbury, T., & O'Boyle, I. (Eds.). (2017). *Understanding sport management: International perspectives.* Taylor & Francis.

Brand, G. (2015). *How the Bosman rule changed football—20 years on* [e-reader version]. https://www.skysports.com/football/news/11095/10100134/how-the-bosman-rule-changed-football-20-years-on

broodje80. (2012). *Italy v Chile World Cup 1962: The battle of Santiago.* https://www.youtube.com/watch?v=T5jVMSlpZhg

Brooks, R. A. (1990). Elephants don't play chess. *Robotics and Autonomous Systems, 6*(12), 3–15.

Buddhapriya, S. (2013). Diversity management practices in select firms in India: A critical analysis. *Indian Journal of Industrial Relations, 48* (4) 597–610.

Bühler, A. W. (2006). *Professional football sponsorship in the English Premier League and the German Bundesliga.* University of Plymouth.

Chaudhary, S. (2019). *Mahesh Bhupati's beauty & wellness startup Scentials raises ₹25 Cr from Unilever ventures* [e-reader version]. https://www.indianweb2. com/2019/06/24/mahesh-bhupatis-beauty-wellness-startup-scentials-raises%E2%82%B925-cr-from-unilever-ventures/

Chen, J. S., & Garg, P. (2018). Dancing with the stars: Benefits of a star employee's temporary absence for organizational performance. *Strategic Management Journal,* 39(5), 1239–67.

Clarke, D. (2019). *Rondos explained* [e-reader version]. https://bsbproduction.s3.amazonaws.com/portals/25846/ docs/rondo%202%20wecompress.com.pdf

College Sports. (2018). *Sponsorship spending on college athletics to total $1.24 billion in 2017/2018 season* [e-reader version]. https://www.sponsorship.com/Report/2018/03/19/ Sponsorship-Spending-On-College-Athletics-To-Total. aspx

Covell, D., & Walker, S. (2013). *Managing sport organizations: Responsibility for performance.* Routledge.

Davidson, N. (2017). *Famous pro athletes who use mental health coaches* [e-reader version]. https://thriveworks.com/ blog/famous-pro-athletes-who-use-mental-health-coaches

de Brabandere, L., & Iny, A. (2010). Scenarios and creativity: Thinking in new boxes. *Technological Forecasting and Social Change,* 77(9), 1506–12.

Dell, M. O. (2013). *Investor behavior and the hot-hand fallacy* [e-reader version]. http://bcswealth.com/2013/07/23/ investor-behavior-and-the-hot-hand-fallacy/

Dhayanithy, D., & Mukherjee, S. (2020). Network memory, cultural distance and the ebb and flow of international resources: Evidence from 20 years of professional player transfers to big-five European soccer leagues. *European Management Journal,* 38(2), 255–66.

Ducker, J. (2017). *Manchester City in advanced talks with Benfica over world-record £35m deal for goalkeeper Ederson* [e-reader version]. https://www.telegraph.co.uk/football/2017/05/28/manchester-city-advanced-talksbenfica-world-record-35-million/

Edwards, A. R. (2010). Why sport? The development of sport as a policy issue in Title IX of the education amendments of 1972. *Journal of Policy History, 22*(3), 300–36.

ESPN. (n.d.). *All-time money leaders* [e-reader version]. http://www.espn.com/golf/moneylist/_/tour/alltime.

ESPN. (1983). *Result 20th Match, Prudential World Cup at Tunbridge Wells, Jun 18 1983* [e-reader version]. https://www.espncricinfo.com/series/8039/scorecard/65083/india-vs-zimbabwe-20th-match-prudential-worldcup-1983

ESPN. (2017). *Result 2nd semi-final, ICC Women's World Cup at Derby, Jul 20 2017* [e-reader version]. https://www.espncricinfo.com/series/8584/scorecard/1085974/australia-women-vs-india-women-2nd-semi-final-iccwomens-world-cup-2017

ESPN. (2020). *'India five years behind Australia and England'— Harmanpreet Kaur*. https://www.espncricinfo.com/story/_/id/28974903/india-domestic-structure-five-years-australiaengland-harmanpreet-kaur

Fernandez, N. (2020). *Fortnite vs PUBG: Ten mobile differences between the two biggest battle royales* [e-reader version]. https://www.androidauthority.com/fortnite-vs-pubg-mobile-861592/

Fischer, K. (2018). *Women's Tennis Association media guide* [e-reader version]. http://wtafiles.wtatennis.com/pdf/publications/2018WTAGuide_lowres.pdf.

Gardiner, E. N. (1906). The pankration and wrestling. III. *The Journal of Hellenic Studies, 26,* 4–22.

Gillmeister, H. (2000). The tale of little Franz and big Franz: The foundation of Bayern Munich FC. *Soccer & Society, 1*(2), 80–106.

Gilovich, T., Vallone, R., & Tversky, A. (1985). The hot hand in basketball: On the misperception of random sequences. *Cognitive Psychology*, *17*(3), 295–314.

Granovetter, M. (1983). The strength of weak ties: A network theory revisited. *Sociological Theory*, *1*, 201–33.

Green, B., & Zwiebel, J. (2018). The hot-hand fallacy: Cognitive mistakes or equilibrium adjustments? Evidence from major league baseball. *Management Science*, *64*(11), 5315–48.

Gündüz, Ş. (2018). Preventing blue ocean from turning into red ocean: A case study of a room escape game. *Journal of Human Sciences*, *15*(1), 1–7.

Gupta, N. (2019). *Women in science and technology: Confronting inequalities*. SAGE Publications.

Gupta, N. (2020). *Indian IT industry attracts more women, but many exit within first 5 years in the job* [e-reader version]. https://theprint.in/pageturner/excerpt/indian-it-industryattracts-more-women-but-many-exit-within-first-5-yearsin-the-job/368504/

Harkins, R. (2017). *To change is to change twice* [e-reader version]. http://asq.org/quality-progress/2017/10/career-corner/to-change-is-to-change-twice.html

Harvard, J. (2002). *Harvard–Yale boat race turns 150* [e-reader version]. https://harvardmagazine.com/2002/05/harvardyale-boat-race-t.html

Hastorf, A. H., & Cantril, H. (1954). They saw a game; A case study. *The Journal of Abnormal and Social Psychology*, *49*(1), 129.

Hindustan Times. (2020). *BCCI central contracts: Know how much Virat Kohli, Rohit Sharma and other Indian cricketers will earn* [e-reader version]. https://www.hindustantimes.com/cricket/bcci-central-contracts-know-how-muchvirat-kohli-rohit-sharma-and-other-indian-cricketerswill-earn/story-CMMWrbEPQDqP9roFDaWqNO.html#:~:text=BCCI%20contracts%3A%20The%20 contracts%2C%20from,C%20(Rs%201%20 crore).&text=The%20Board%20of%20Control%20 for,Team%20India%20(Senior%20Men

IIMK. (2020). *About executive post graduate programmes (EPGP)* [e-reader version]. https://www.iimk.ac.in/ academics/epgp/aboutmain.php

ISHOF. (2020). *Anthony Nesty (SUR) honor swimmer* [e-reader version]. https://ishof.org/anthony-nesty-(sur).html

Isusports. (2015). *Madelene Sagström 2014–15: Women's golf—LSU Tigers* [e-reader version]. https://lsusports. net/sports/womens-golf/roster/madelene-Sagström/ 3631

Janoff, B. (2018). *State farm ensures sponsor spend on college sports hits record $1.24B in 2018* [e-reader version]. http:// nysportsjournalism.squarespace.com/brands-top-1bspend- in-college/2018/3/15/state-farm-ensures-sponsorspend-on- college-sports-hits-reco.html

Jat, A. (2020). Unfair to demand, women's team not a World Champion yet: Anjum Chopra on pay parity in Indian cricket [e-reader version]. *India Today.* https://www.indiatoday.in/sports/cricket/story/unfair- todemand-anjum-chopra-on-gender-pay-gap-india- cricket-1661295-2020-03-30

Kahan, D. M., Hoffman, D. A., Braman, D., & Evans, D. (2012). They saw a protest: Cognitive illiberalism and the speechconduct distinction. *The Stanford Law Review*, 64, 851.

Kim, W. C., & Mauborgne, R. (2005). Value innovation: A leap into the blue ocean. *Journal of Business Strategy*, 26(4), 22–28.

Kleinert, J., Ohlert, J., Carron, B., Eys, M., Feltz, D., Harwood, C., Linz, L., Seiler, R., & Sulprizio, M. (2012). Group dynamics in sports: An overview and recommendations on diagnostic and intervention. *The Sport Psychologist*, 26(3), 412–34.

Koch, L. (2019). *E-sports playing in the Big Leagues now* [e-reader version]. https://www.emarketer.com/content/e-sports-disrupts-digital-sports-streaming

Korth, S. J. (2000). Single and double-loop learning: Exploring potential influence of cognitive style. *Organization Development Journal*, 18(3), 87.

Lange, D. (2020). *Total transfer fee spending of big-5 league football clubs from 2010 to 2019* [e-reader version]. https://www.statista.com/statistics/742926/big-5-soccer-league-transfer-fee-spending/.

Lebell, G. (1963). *Handbook of judo*. Simon & Schuster.

Lewis, M. (2003). *Moneyball: The art of winning an unfair game*. W. W. Norton & Company.

Lindgren, P., Saghaug, K. M., & Clemmensen, S. (2010). The pitfalls of the blue ocean strategy implications of 'the Six Paths Framework'. In *11th International CINet ConferencePracticing Innovation in Times of Discontinuity*. https://vbn.aau.dk/en/publications/the-pitfalls-of-the-blue-oceanstrategy-implications-of-the-six-p

Lovallo, D., & Mendonca, L. (2007). *Strategy's strategist: An interview with Richard Rumelt* [e-reader version]. https://www.mckinsey.com/business-functions/strategy-andcorporate-finance/our-insights/strategys-strategist-an-interview-with-richard-rumelt#

Luo, L., Yang, X. C., & Gong, M. J. (2013). The research on Barcelona and Spain Tiki-Taka football style. *Journal of Hebei Institute of Physical Education* (3), 13.

Magretta, J. (2011). *Understanding Michael Porter: The essential guide to competition and strategy*. Harvard Business Press.

Maher, B. S. (2009). Understanding and regulating the sport of mixed martial arts. *Hastings Communications and Entertainment Law Journal*, 32(2), 209.

Manola, S. (2019). *Loss aversion strategies to dial-up your ecommerce conversion* [e-reader version]. https://www.abtasty.com/blog/loss-aversion

Mansfield, L., Wheaton, B., Caudwell, J., & Watson, R. (2017). *Sportswomen still face sexism, but feminism can help achieve a level playing field* [e-reader version]. https://scroll.in/field/845726/sportswomen-still-face-sexism-butfeminism-can-help-achieve-a-level-playing-field

Masucci, M., & Butryn, T. M. (2013). Writing about fighting: A critical content analysis of newspaper coverage of the Ultimate Fighting Championship from 1993–2006. *Journal of Sports Media*, *8*(1), 19–44.

Mauborgne, R., & Kim, W. C. (2005). Blue ocean strategy. *Harvard Business Review*, *1*, 256.

MBTA. (2015). *About us* [e-reader version]. https://www.mbtaworld.com/about.php

McMahon, B. (2015). *Why the Bosman ruling never brought the chaos so many predicted* [e-reader version]. https://www.forbes.com/sites/bobbymcmahon/2015/12/15/thethreat-of-players-using-the-bosman-rule-has-been-morepowerful-than-invoking-it/#c7b85a320043

McVeigh, N., Christenson, M., & Blight, G. (2019, 4 June). Transfer window summer 2019—Every deal from Europe's top five leagues [e-reader version]. *The Guardian*. https://www.theguardian.com/football/ng-interactive/2019/jun/04/football-transfer-window-2019-every-summerdeal-from-europe-top-five-leagues

Mintzberg, H. (1987). The strategy concept I: Five Ps for strategy. *California Management Review*, *30*(1), 11–24.

Mitra, S. (2010). The IPL: India's foray into world sports business. *Sport in Society*, *13*(9), 1314–33.

Monster India.com. (2017). *Monster salary index* [e-reader version]. https://my.monsterindia.com/salary-check.html

Murphy, D. (2020). *Former Bayern Munich goalkeeper reveals what Man City boss Pep Guardiola is like at training* [e-reader version]. https://www.manchestereveningnews.co.uk/sport/football/man-city-pep-guardiola-ederson-17974279

NCAA. (2018–2019). *National Collegiate Athletic*

Association consolidated financial statements [e-reader version]. https://ncaaorg.s3.amazonaws.com/ncaa/finance/201819NCAAFin_NCAAFinancials.pdf

Neyer, R. (2016). *Sabermetrics* [e-reader version]. https://www.britannica.com/biography/Bill-James

Northcroft, J. (2016). *Fearless: The amazing underdog story of Leicester City, the greatest miracle in sports history.* Hachette.

Northouse, P. G. (2007). Transformational leadership. In *Leadership: Theory and Practice* (4th ed., pp. 175–206). SAGE Publications.

Pal, S. (2019). Past perfect, present continuous, future tense. In Robert J. Lake (Ed.), *Routledge handbook of tennis: History, culture and politics.* Taylor & Francis Group.

Paulsen. (2020). *Ratings: NFL on CBS, Lakers-Warriors, WNBA Finals, MLS* [e-reader version]. https://www.sportsmediawatch.com/2019/10/nfl-cbs-ratings-nba-lakers-warriors-wnba-mls/

Payscale.com. (2020). *The state of the gender pay gap 2020* [e-reader version]. https://www.payscale.com/data/gender-pay-gap

Pope, D. G., & Schweitzer, M. E. (2011). Is Tiger Woods loss averse? Persistent bias in the face of experience, competition, and high stakes. *American Economic Review, 101*(1), 129–57.

Portsche, M. (2019). *Obstacles faced by women in sports* [e-reader version]. https://medium.com/womens-sports/obstacles-faced-by-women-in-sports-813285cb544c

Posner, B. Z., & Kouzes, J. M. (1988). Relating leadership and credibility. *Psychological Reports, 63*(2), 527–30.

Prahalad, C. K., & Hamel, G. (2006). The core competence of the corporation. In D. Hahn & and B. Taylor (Eds.), *Strategische unternehmungsplanung—Strategische unternehmungsführung* (pp. 275–92). Springer.

Prithingar, K. (2018). *5 Players that defined the last decade of FC Barcelona* [e-reader version]. https://www.sportskeeda.

com/football/5-players-that-defined-the-last-decade-offc-barcelona/2

PTI. (2019a). *Gender pay gap still high, women in India earn 19% less than men: Report* [e-reader version]. https://www.livemint.com/industry/human-resource/gender-paygap-still-high-women-in-india-earn-19-less-than-menreport-1551948081615.html

PTI. (2019b). *Mary sets sight on Olympics after world championship bronze* [e-reader version]. https://www.rediff.com/sports/report/mary-sets-sight-on-olympics-after-worldsbronze/20191012.htm

PTI. (2020). *Massive jump in number of Indian students going to UK universities* [e-reader version]. https://www.financialexpress.com/education-2/massive-jump-in-number-of-indianstudents-going-to-uk-universities/1826881/

Ray, S. (2016). *Challenges faced by female athletes in the world of sports* [e-reader version]. https://yourstory.com/2016/09/challenges-female-athletes-face

Rittenberg, A. (2014). *Big ten to guarantee scholarships* [e-reader version]. https://www.espn.in/college-sports/story/_/id/11666316/big-ten-guarantees-four-year-scholarships-student-athletes

Romo Flores, A. (2020). What makes a good loser? An ethnographic study of toxic behaviors in competitive multiplayer games (Dissertation, Digitala Vetenskapliga Arkivet). http://www.diva-portal.org/smash/record.jsf?pid=diva2%3A1445944&dswid=-3568

Ronay, B. (2020). *Handshakes, dark suits and money-glaze: Welcome to the Mendes supremacy* [e-reader version]. https://www.theguardian.com/football/blog/2020/jan/17/jorge-mendes-supremacy-portuguese-super-agent-dealsfootball

Salancik, G. R., & Pfeffer, J. (1978). A social information processing approach to job attitudes and task design. *Administrative Science Quarterly*, 23(2), 224–53.

Sankar, R. (2020). *BCCI could take a cue from Australia on how to treat women's team* [e-reader version]. https://www.thequint.com/sports/sports-specials/how-cricket-australiatreats-its-women-cricketers-equal-pay-benefits

Sapatwala, M. (2020). *Is India ready to embrace the need of women sports managers?* [e-reader version]. https://www.iismworld.com/is-india-ready-to-embrace-the-need-of-womensports-managers/#:~:text=In%20Indian%20sports%20 association%20governing, representation%2C%20is%20 the%20only%20exception

Schön, D., & Argyris, C. (1996). *Organizational learning II: Theory, method and practice.* Addison Wesley.

Schultz, J. (2011). The physical activism of Billie Jean King. In S. Wagg (Ed.), *Myths and milestones in the history of sport* (pp. 203–23). Palgrave Macmillan.

Schwarz, A. (2009). *Settling for par: Pros more likely to play it safe* [e-reader version]. https://www.nytimes.com/2009/06/16/sports/golf/16study.html.

Septiana, R. M. R. (2019). The violation of politeness principle in the case study of UFC 229 press conferences: Khabib vs McGregor (Doctoral dissertation, UIN Sunan Gunung Djati Bandung).

Shiff, B. (2017). *The history behind America's oldest active collegiate sporting event* [e-reader version]. https://abcnews.go.com/Sports/history-americas-oldest-active-collegiate-sporting-event/story?id= 47852376

Siegel, J., & Chang, J. J. (2005). *Samsung electronics* [e-reader version]. https://hbsp.harvard.edu/product/705508-PDF-ENG

Snowden, J. (2016). *For Dana White and Fertittas, UFC sale leaves behind complex legacy* [e-reader version]. https://bleacherreport.com/articles/2651522-for-dana-white-andfertittas-ufc-sale-leavesbehind-complex-legacy

Soriano, F. (2012). *Goal: The ball doesn't go in by chance* (pp. 94–115). Palgrave Macmillan.

Sotiriadou, P., & Haan, D. D. (2019). Women and leadership: advancing gender equity policies in sport leadership through sport governance. *International Journal of Sport Policy and Politics, 11*(3), 365–83. https://www.tandfonline.com/doi/abs/10.1080/19406940.2019.1577902?src=recsys&journalCode=risp20

Sports Bureau. (2017). *Guardiola's style is total football: Neeskens* [e-reader version]. https://www.thehindu.com/sport/football/guardiolas-style-is-total-football-neeskens/article19941636.ece

Stephanie, J. (2017). *11 quotes from Billie Jean King that will inspire you to persevere* [e-reader version]. https://medium.com/thrive-global/11-quotes-from-billie-jean-king-thatwill-inspire-you-to-persevere-ea4066dbd35e

Taylor, B. (2018). *What breaking the 4-minute mile taught us about the limits of conventional thinking* [e-reader version]. https://hbr.org/2018/03/what-breaking-the-4-minutemile-taught-us-about-the-limits-of-conventional-thinking

Transfermarket. (n.d.). *Gestifute: Player agency—Player agents* [e-reader version]. https://www.transfermarkt.com/gestifute/beraterfirma/berater/413/plus/1

U. S. Department of Education. (2015). *Title IX and sex discrimination* [e-reader version]. https://www2.ed.gov/about/offices/list/ocr/docs/tix_dis.html#:~:text=Title%20IX%20states%20that%3A,activity%20receiving%20Federal%20financial%20assistance

Violan, M. Á. (2014). *Pep Guardiola: The philosophy that changed the game.* Meyer & Meyer Verlag.

Waxman, O. (2018). *She exposed the discrimination in college sports before Title IX. Now she's a women's history month honoree* [e-reader version]. https://time.com/5175812/title-ix-sports-womens-history

West, R. F., Meserve, R. J., & Stanovich, K. E. (2012). Cognitive sophistication does not attenuate the bias blind spot. *Journal of Personality and Social Psychology*, *103*(3), 506.

White, D. E. (2015). Arthur Ashe: Tennis and justice in the civil rights era. *The Journal of Southern History*, *81*(4), 1044.

Wilson, W. V. (Ed.). (1991). *Coverage of women's sports in four daily newspapers*. Amateur Athletic Foundation of Los Angeles.

Yagi, K., Funayama, T., & Yamamoto, Y. (2014, November). The digitizing of the characteristic and visualization of the wave of the condition of batter of the professional baseball. In *2014 Twelfth International Conference on ICT and Knowledge Engineering* (pp. 43–47). IEEE.

Yüksel, I. (2012). Developing a multi-criteria decision making model for PESTEL analysis. *International Journal of Business and Management*, *7*(24), 52.

Ziemnowicz, C. (2013). *Joseph A. Schumpeter and innovation* [e-reader version]. https://link.springer.com/referencewo rkentry/10.1007%2F978-1-4614-3858-8_476